CReaTinG
aRT
FROM
anyTHinG

Dona Z. meiLaCH

iDeas
maTeRiaLs
TeCHniques

REILLY & LEE • CHICAGO

For Julius Zweigoron, my father, who taught us to apply our imaginations to the visible world around us.

Other Books by Dona Z. Meilach

COLLAGE AND FOUND ART
with Elvie Ten Hoor

CREATING WITH PLASTER

DIRECT METAL SCULPTURE
with Donald Seiden

HOW TO MAKE RUGS AND WALL HANGINGS

PAPERCRAFT

PRINTMAKING

Foreword

Creating Art from Anything is a comprehensive survey of the use in the arts of easily accessible non-art material. By example and instruction, the book is designed to stimulate readers of every age to broaden their awareness of the expressive potential of mundane materials.

The ideas and techniques in this book are offered by students and artists who have an uncanny ability to transpose the materials they live with into arresting artistic statements. Although one artist may prefer one technique, each emphasizes that there are no rigid rules, no one best technique or way to use the materials. Each person must experiment and develop his individual preferences. The ultimate achievement is originality and inventiveness in bringing assorted items into compositions that are aesthetic and appealing to the eye, the mind and the heart.

Most of the techniques shown in this book are basically so simple, and the materials so accessible, that they can be used in the classroom with youngsters from the early grades on up. Therefore I have devoted no one special chapter to classroom projects; almost all of them in this book are suitable for this purpose.

The techniques and examples are both by and for the art student and educator, professional artist, hobbyist and craftsman, whose ingenuity is helping to splinter artistic expression in sparkling new directions.

Acknowledgments

A book such as this owes its being to the generosity of the artists, teachers and students who contributed their works and photographs. Private art collectors, museum and gallery directors combed their collections to select the best examples of this particular art form. Listing credits is discharging only a small part of my indebtedness to them.

I am especially grateful to the artists who spent hours under hot floodlights demonstrating their techniques as I hovered about them with my camera and tape recorder.

I want to express my appreciation to the educators, students and schools who made work available for my camera. These include: Tom Harris, Skiles Junior High School, Evanston, Illinois; Anita Gorr and Chuck Visgatis, Deerfield High School, Deerfield, Illinois; Tom Blackburn, Niles West High School, Skokie, Illinois; Ray Pearson, Institute of Design, Illinois Institute of Technology, Chicago, Illinois; Jeff Donaldson, Northeastern Illinois State College (N.I.S.C.), Chicago; and John Walley, University of Illinois at the Chicago Circle Campus. Special thanks to David C. Huntley, professor of art, Southern Illinois University, Edwardsville, Illinois, who developed the series of photos on plastics.

My endless gratitude to Ben Lavit of Astra Photo, Inc., Chicago, who worked with me on the development and overall consistency of photographs. Most of all, my thanks to my husband, Dr. Melvin Meilach, who, as always, lends enthusiasm and encouragement to my projects as well as a strong back for transporting my camera equipment.

Dona Z. Meilach
Chicago, Illinois

Note: Photographs by the author unless otherwise credited.

Contents

creating
art
from
anything

1. TIME, CHANCE AND FORTUNE, *Sand Fountain #28, Ann Wiseman.* Clock parts, an abacus, coins and sand within a glass box with a walnut frame.
Collection, The Chase Manhattan Bank, New York

1 Creating Art from Anything

Today when one approaches a painting or a sculpture, it isn't always easy to determine its components. A picture no longer is made up only of oil paints, pastels or watercolors; it may have many real objects on its surface. Sculptures, traditionally made of stone or bronze, are now composed of anything and everything, so that a sculpture is simply an art form that exists in space in three dimensions. Artists have employed non-traditional materials in their work since the early 1900's, but in the last decade or so the widespread use of such objects has thrown art into a state of vital ferment.

The materials used by the contemporary artist are the materials of his environment. He often expresses the way he lives through the real objects he uses in his art. These objects may range from sunbaked old shoes, plastic containers, delicately textured fabrics, gears and scraps of metal to nature's objects such as seeds, feathers, butterflies, branches, shells and bones. The artist is concerned with everything about him, his relation to it and its relation to him.

In the past, art was something separated from life. A painting or sculpture was placed in a museum where people went to visit it on a Sunday. Today we surround ourselves with art in every aspect of our environment from the commercials we view to the buildings we inhabit.

When an artist selects an object to use in a painting or a sculpture, it usually has specific connotations for him personally. He may choose it because of its function. It may initially evoke an emotional response. He may even become so involved that he hates to part with the item. The object may remind him of something or someone. It may simply appeal to his senses or to his intellect and he wonders what will happen to it when he puts it into a new context. For the concern of the artist is to create orderly form while changing the relationships of objects to produce sensual, emotional or intellectual reactions.

It is the ability to visualize and communicate a metamorphosis that makes one an artist. For example, a person looking at a bare tree may see only the bare tree, but the artist may see it as a dancing figure with graceful, moving lines. He may see not only the bare branches as moving arms; he may observe the shape of sky enclosed by those branches and thus the tree appears changed to him as the result of its new relationship to space.

When Pablo Picasso and Georges Braque first began placing real objects on their canvases in the early 1900's, the concept was referred to as "junk art" or "found object art." Not so in today's context. Though many objects used may be considered junk or scraps of our waste society, they are carefully *selected* by the artist for the potential they have to evoke emotion through change into an art form.

As artists employ non-traditional materials they face many technical problems. Paints, brushes, chisels and clays have to be supplemented with industrial products. To fuse metal, soldering and welding equipment are becoming standard items in the sculptor's studio. Those who work with wood find that carpenter's tools are essential, both hand and power varieties. A wide range of adhesives must be explored for joining like and unlike materials.

By combining art techniques along with those of industry, the artist glues, constructs and assembles. All these techniques expressed themselves in the gamut of art movements that have developed in the twentieth century: Cubism, Dadaism, Surrealism, through pop, op and Funk art.

Ironically, we consider the use of selected materials from every conceivable source as a contemporary revolution in art. Yet primitive man used the products of his environment for centuries. African ceremonial masks are made of human hair, woven cane fibers and feathers. The fringe of a South American ceremonial skirt is composed of hollow bird bones strung together and edged with tiny monkey teeth and the irridescent green wings from large beetles. A decorative necklace is made of toucan bills; rattles are composed of deer hooves, tortoise shells and seashells. Today's artists find natural history museums a source of inspiration for form, design and combinations of materials.

It is impossible to predict where the trend to creating art from anything will lead. What can be predicted is that the artist and the viewer will continue to recognize their dependency upon their environment and its effect on them. And this will be re-flected in the art. It is important to appreciate and understand the artist's concern; for through this concern with the materials of his surroundings, he attempts to turn the environment for all of us into an artistic milieu by understanding the everyday forms and translating them into art. The artist does not randomly and without thinking gather materials and assemble them. His sensitivity to his environment causes him to select and assemble things critically.

Those who wish to express their own sensations and personal observations by transforming objects into new relationships will find the following pages filled with examples that stimulate awareness of the artistic qualities of a staggering variety of materials.

2. GALLOPING STICKS. Popsicle sticks become a sculptural expression when glued into a rhythmic arrangement.

Student, Skiles Jr. High

3. ORGANIC STUDY, *Fred Borcherdt*

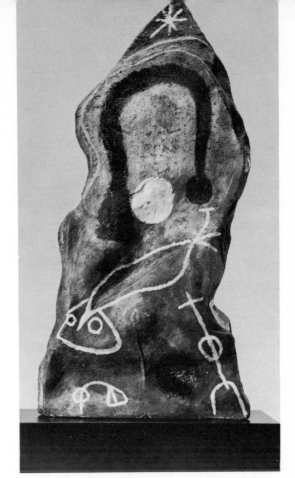

4. STONE, *Joàn Miro*
Courtesy, The Art Institute of Chicago

5. SCREENING, *Alice Faber*
Student, University of Illinois, Chicago
Circle Campus
Photo: John Walley

3.—The crease and small knot form within a large knot from a mahogany tree is mounted without any additional work by the artist.

4.—A glazed ceramic design was added to the natural stone shape.

5.—Ordinary screen wire has the appearance of a drawing in space. It is bent and twisted to suggest volume, yet has a transparent effect.

Materials

The materials used in the examples throughout the book are among the least expensive and most readily available of those for any art form. Pebbles picked up on a beach, wood from forest preserves, parts from an old clock, a box of straws—these cost very little if anything at all. Minimal expense is incurred for the backings and the glues. The more involved procedures such as woodworking and welding may be accomplished with inexpensive hand tools; the serious enthusiast may wish to graduate to more sophisticated welding equipment and power tools.

With a little imagination almost anything you have around the house may be used for a first art experience with mundane materials. Suitable backings for a relief assemblage would be a piece of canvas board, masonite or plywood.

The materials used to adhere one object to another or to a mounting board will depend upon the object. There are dozens of glues especially compounded for materials that range from thin, delicate papers and fabrics to heavy pieces of iron (see the glue chart on page 119. Every material can be adhered by some glue. If you find that an all-purpose glue is unsatisfactory for a particular project, experiment with other compounds on the market. Consult the labels and follow instructions carefully for best results.

There are four basic ways to combine materials.

1. Gluing: This includes polyvinyl resin white glues, contact cements, household glues and epoxies. Library paste and rubber cement should be used mainly with papers.

2. Bolting, nailing and screwing: Used for metals and woods. Sometimes glues are combined with these techniques for greater solidity and permanence.

3. Stitching: Used with fabrics. May also be combined with glue.

4. Soldering, welding: With these methods the molecular makeup of the materials is altered by the application of heat.

All these techniques with variations are demonstrated in the following chapters.

If you try to remember that creating art from anything is not a "purist" art form with only one way to use any one technique or combination of materials, you will be able to give wider range to your own expressiveness. Traditional oil paints, temperas and acrylic-base paints may be combined with non-traditional materials. There are no rules to bind the creative energy other than those of pleasing design, color combination and composition. Even then, rules of design are not strict. The best way to begin is to select some materials around the house and see them with an inventive eye and a new awareness of their form and pattern. Then squeeze out some glue and set to work, as the artist has done in the three photographs on the following page.

6. Glues

7.

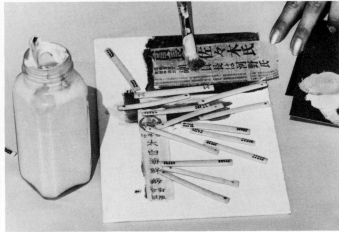

8.

9. MAH-JONGG, *Dona Meilach*

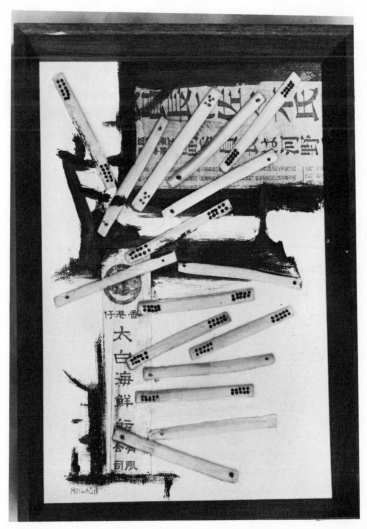

7.—Old ivory Mah-Jongg money with the repeated dots in black and red suggested parts for an interesting composition. A piece of oriental newspaper, a canvas board, paint, glue and a frame are the simple materials.

8.—Shapes of color were painted on the board first, then the tiles and paper glued on in a simple arrangement. Thin paper can be glued through from the top as well as from the bottom. A piece of cardboard served as the palette for the water-base acrylic paints.

9.—After the objects were glued to the backboard, the artist added more paint in shapes repeating the oriental letters. Framing was done last, after paint dried.

10. THE JOKER, *Jean Dubuffet*. A coal clinker mounted on stone and lightly carved.

Collection, Mr. and Mrs. Arnold Maremont, Winnetka, Illinois

2 Art from Nature's Objects

Artistic awareness begins when you learn to look at an object and see beyond its original function. This awareness develops as you train yourself to observe the patterns and forms inherent in objects. One way to begin developing this awareness as a habit is to think visually, in terms of a picture or composition, when you look at a product of nature. You may be amazed at how much you have missed.

Everyone recognizes that a flower has inherent natural beauty. The texture of a rose petal almost begs you to feel its softness. An animal's fur is pleasing to the touch and to the eye. But what about things in nature not usually associated with beauty? They too may have qualities that appeal to the senses of the viewer. Barnacles, tenaciously attached to a pier, catch sunlight, shadow and water reflections to reveal interesting patterns in their growth. The shell of a snail spirals with lines of color. A stone, washed smooth by the surf, may cause you to pick it up and rub it with your thumb. The feel of sand sifting through your fingers may relate to a feeling of timelessness. The veining on a leaf may have symbolism for you.

Many of nature's castoffs can be mounted and used as sculpture in their natural state. Others may require minimal sculpting or combining with compatible objects.

11. MASK, *Ambryn Island, New Hebrides*. Hemp, fibers, bark, traces of color.
Courtesy, The Art Institute of Chicago

12. *Collection, Robert Bailey, Chicago*

12.—Tree barks have textures which we are accustomed to seeing. But the inside of a piece of bark has patterns and textures that few people think of noticing. There are tiny holes, cracks and fossil-like designs, as this piece of bark shows.

13.—With a face carved into it, a dried tree root becomes a humorous human form.

14.—The protrusions, texture, tone and general shape of a piece of found natural wood have the qualities of sculpture in the natural state.

13. *Collection, Dr. and Mrs. Meilach*

14. *Collection, Dr. and Mrs. Meilach*

15.—Seashells and sand-smoothed pieces of sun-dried driftwood arranged flat and on end in a simple wooden box.

16.—This plant, found in a forest preserve, has negative spaces between the forms that are as interesting as the plant itself.

17.—A single bone from the vertebrae of a cow suggested the animal form. Slight carving, ball bearings for eyes and burnt sienna paint completed the illusion.

15. UNTITLED, *Robert Pierron*
Collection, Dr. and Mrs. Melvin Meilach

16. *Collection, Robert Bailey, Chicago*

17. WILD BOAR, *Robert Pierron*

18. SAND FOUNTAIN WITH ANTIQUE MIRROR AND GARNET SAND, *Ann Wiseman*. Wooden box with plexiglass separations holds sand, bleached driftwood and seashells.

Collection, The Chase Manhattan Bank, New York

19. HUMAN FORM, *Agnese Udinotti*. Cow dung baked and hardened by the sun in the Arizona desert.
Courtesy of the artist

20. HARPY LISTENING, *John R. Baxter.* Stone and wood.

   Courtesy, San Francisco Museum of Art

21. FAIR HARBOR, *Anita Weschler.* Stone and wood.

   Courtesy, Sculptors Guild, Inc., New York

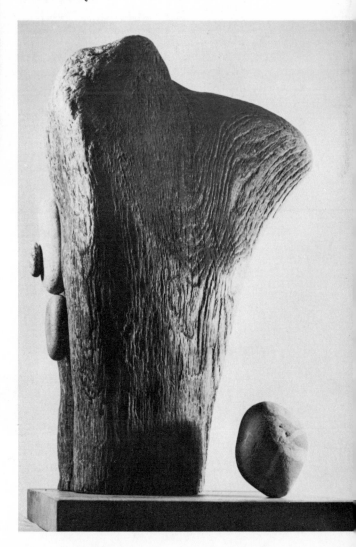

14

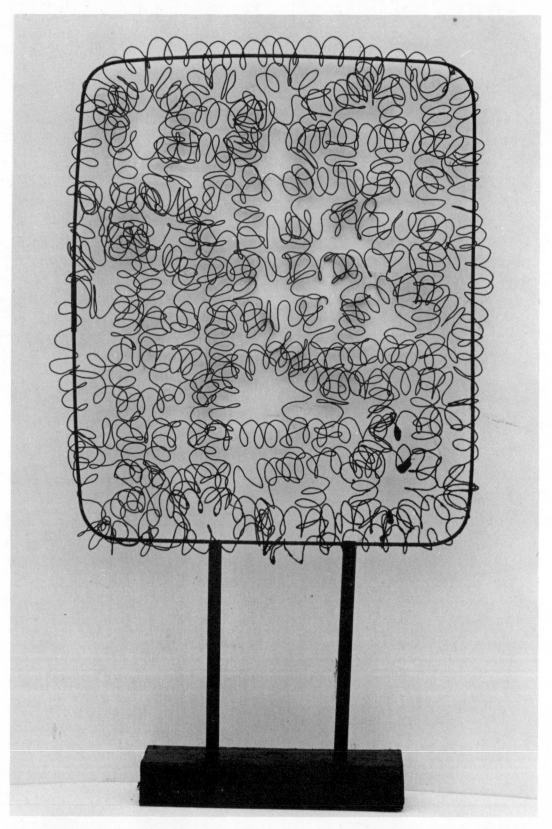

22. INTERNAL REARRANGEMENT, *Dona Meilach*. The innerspring of a car seat mashed by traffic is now a sculpture.

28. LEANING TOWER, *Linda Luckenbach.*
Sculpture of cotton swab sticks.
Student, N. I. S. C., Chicago

29. RELIEF DESIGN, *Sharon Wolkey.*
Cotton swab sticks.
Student, N. I. S. C., Chicago

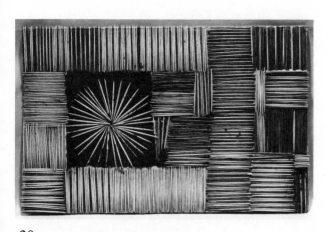

30. TOOTHPICK ARRANGEMENT
Student, Skiles Jr. High

31. TOOTHPICK SCULPTURE, *Steve Kushner.*
Student, N. I. S. C., Chicago

32. A STRAINED MAN, *Robert Bailey*

32.—A broken, useless strainer filled in and molded in relief with modeling paste, painted and mounted. The face can be turned in the holder to give a variety of humorous positions to the sculpture.

33.—The strainer wire is pushed in and the face built up by using modeling paste, plaster or plastic metal that dries hard in a few minutes.

34.—Features may be added using anything available. Thread and yarn are embedded in the wet paste to represent hair. Eyes are tiny rubber furniture tips. The handle will be inserted into the plastic dish filled with plaster to form the base. The entire piece will be painted.

33.

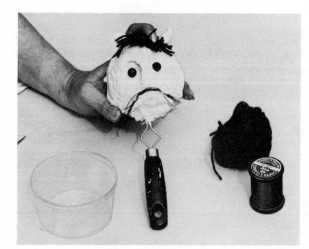

34.

35. POPSICLE STICKS
Student, Skiles Jr. High

36. WOOD PADDLE STICKS
Student, Skiles Jr. High

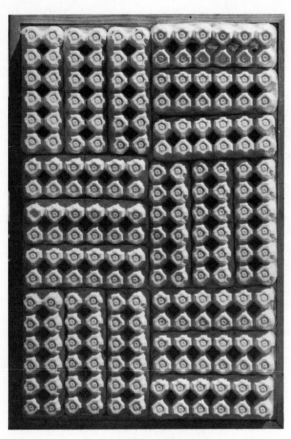

37. EGG CASE CONSTRUCTION, *Donna Ryan*
Student, Deerfield High School

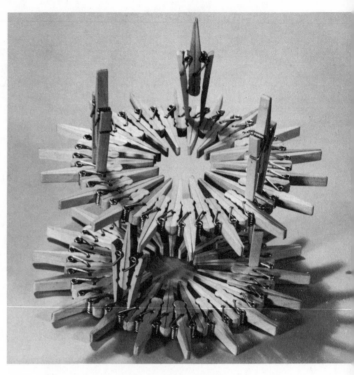

38. CLOTHESPIN SCULPTURE, *Stephen Lehtman*
Student, N. I. S. C., Chicago

39. CLOTHESPIN HILL
Student, Skiles Jr. High

40. COLORED SPONGECRAFT
Student, Skiles Jr. High

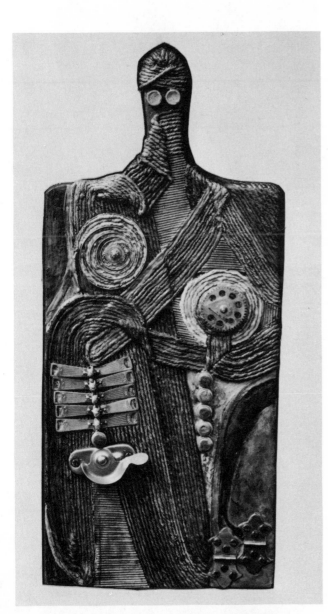

42. IN EFFIGY, *Robert Borchard*.
Jar, can, pressed cardboard cone and
straight pins.

*Collection, Lester Rebbeck, Ar-
lington Heights, Illinois*

41. BOLDER SOLDIER, *Rubin Steinberg*.
Rope, clock parts, zipper tabs, locks, hinges,
buttons mounted on a breadboard and covered with polymer medium for a preservative.

43. FAMILY GROUP, *Jacob Burck*. Wooden spoons and bowls assembled in a humorous relationship become people. Eyes and nose are pieces of the cut-off handle.
Courtesy, Conrad Gallery, Chicago

44. FRAGMENTED SPOONS. By cutting the spoon bowls with a saw and putting them together in a new relationship, a sculpture results.

Student, Institute of Design, I. I. T., Chicago

45. COME TO THE PICNIC, *Maureen Clark Student, N. I. S. C., Chicago*

46. SPAGHETTI, *L. Goodman*. A fork wound with wire suggests realism and humor.
  Photo: Helfant

47. FORK ARRANGEMENT, *Judith A. Janik*
  Student, N. I. S. C., Chicago

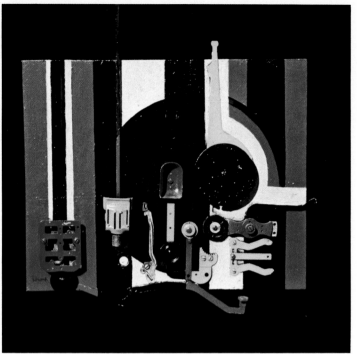

CIRCLE AND STRIPE, *Ralph Arnold*. Typewriter keys, mechanical parts, acrylic paint
 Photo: Dona Meilach

ARKANSAS, *Enrique Riverón*. Mixed media, including nails, screening, can lids, wood, car tailpipe

KACHINA III, *Claude Bentley*. Fabric, acrylic paint
 Photo: Dona Meilach

FEMME FATALE, *Robert Pierron*. Soldered silverware parts, driftwood, wooden boxes
 Photo: Dona Meilach

48. HIGH RISE. Hair rollers and picks.
Student, N. I. S. C., Chicago

49. CEREBRAL BONES, *Mary Ann Zichittella*. The insides from permanent hair curlers have bone-like forms.
Student, N. I. S. C., Chicago

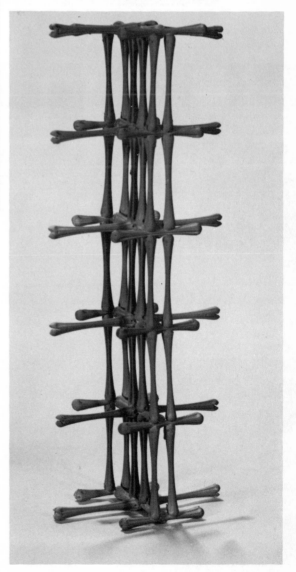

50.

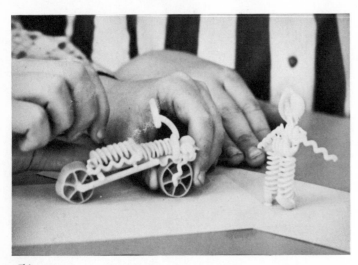

51.

52.

There is a rich harvest of art materials in many food items. You can build sculptures from noodles, from solidly shaped breakfast cereals, from pretzels, straight and knotted. Lima beans, split peas, coffee beans, rice, barley and other raw foods are all potential art media. Creating sculptures from food products is a regular assignment in art classrooms. The object is to alert students to interesting shapes in their everyday environment and to stimulate them to imagine how the items may be transformed.

Noodles with a great variety of shapes have been used in the examples on these two pages.

Appealing shapes of pasta, shells, elbows, etc. trigger creative ingenuity. The creators of these two sculptures, students from Warrensburg-Latham Jr. High, Warrensburg, Illinois, have dubbed their products "noodle art." (Photos by Edith Brockway)

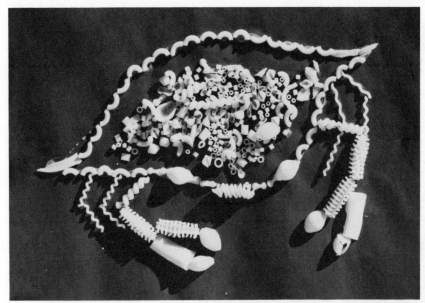

53. CRAB

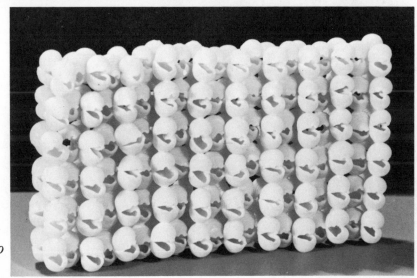

54. SHELL CONSTRUCTION,
Carmen Perez
    Student, N. I. S. C., Chicago

55. HOT ROD. Pasta wheels, rotoni for motor parts and macaroni lengths for understructure.
   Photo: Edith Brockway

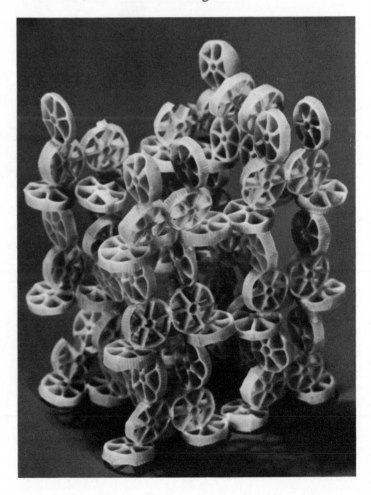

57. PASTA WHEELS
Student, N. I. S. C., Chicago

56. GRANNY BEAN, *Christie Ommen.* Assorted types, shapes and sizes of beans have been ingeniously combined with fabrics and paint in this three-dimensional collage.
Student, Deerfield High School

58. BROWN EYE, WHY ARE YOU BLUE?, *Robert Pierron*. Arrangement of objects on a plate gives the appearance of a plate of food. Objects are a glass eye, sea coral, nut shells and a variety of seashells embedded in epoxy glue which resembles sauce.

59. ASSEMBLAGE, *Claude Bentley.* Cotton sheeting, burlap, hemp and other fabrics with varied textures are assembled with corks, nails, pieces of oddly shaped wood and acrylic paint.

Collection, Mr. and Mrs. Philip Spertus, Glencoe, Illinois

4 Collage and Constructions from Cloth

Cloth has infinite range as an expressive material for the artist. Scraps from worn, favorite garments, placed on a surface, can have a deep and lasting emotional impact. They can evoke memories just as the patches of a quilt recalled certain events to our grandmothers who sewed together old pieces of aprons and dresses. Cloth is intimate and warm. It may also have symbolic meaning, from the poverty and degradation found in tattered beggars' burlap to the wealth and sumptuousness suggested by silks and brocades.

Bits of cloth appeared in early folk art, but Pablo Picasso first placed it onto a fine art surface. A piece of real oilcloth that looked like woven cane became the chair in his "Still Life with Chair Caning." In 1914 he used a piece of floral striped weave as the shirt front of "The Smoker." Casimer Malĕvich placed lace and ornamental braid along with paper collage. The fabrics became either symbols or replicas of the real objects, thus assuming different functions in an art context.

Today the artist may use fabrics because he enjoys the feel of the texture or the memory it stirs. He may respond to the pattern or recognize that a certain fabric can be manipulated by itself or in relation to other materials for the message he wishes to convey.

Torn edges, sharply cut edges, soft padding and tails of texture are only a few of the rich surface qualities that can be achieved with fabrics. Soft sculptures are another new application of the use of fabric in art.

Fabrics may be glued with any of the polymer emulsions and white glues, which

60. TALKING IT OVER, *Rubin Steinberg*. An old pair of ladies' gloves are combined with twine and rope. Oil paints are used for features on rope and background.

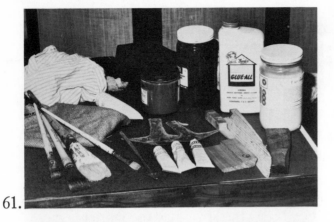

61.

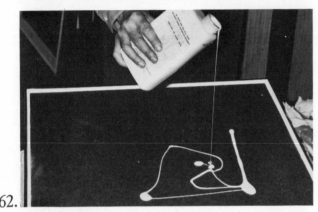

62.

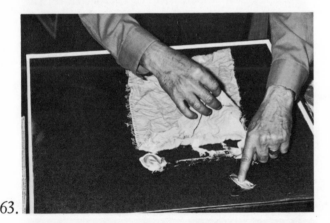

63.

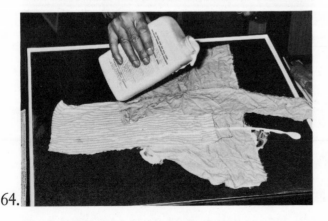

64.

also tend to harden and preserve. By spraying, dousing or brushing cloth with the emulsions, the cloth can be lifted to form three-dimensional shapes.

Many assemblages and constructions combine fabrics with paint, scraps of wood, nails, metal, stitchery and all other media.

Claude Bentley demonstrates the creation of a fabric assemblage.

Assemble the materials—glue, acrylic paints, paint brushes, assorted textiles, pieces of wood and antique Peruvian money (the axe-shaped pieces of metal) (Fig. 61). Mr. Bentley works on masonite set into a "floater" frame (one that has space between the backing and the frame molding). By working within a frame, you get a better idea of your composition. It also reduces possible damage to the surface if the assemblage has to be handled by the framer after it is completed.

Dribble the glue onto the masonite (Fig. 62). Be generous with the glue, for it permeates and hardens the fibers of the cloth.

Place a large shape of fabric on the masonite (Fig. 63). The torn and raveled edges make for greater texture and interest. Add glue under all corners. You may want to burn a hole in a fabric and place another color under the hole to show through.

Build up layers of fabrics of different colors and textures, always aiming for a pleasing composition (Fig. 64). The glue may be poured on top of the materials. It dries clear and hard.

The artist adds a wad of fabric for a higher three-dimensional effect that will ultimately cast interesting and changing shadows as the light plays upon the composition (Fig. 65). This "balled" fabric is simply folded in upon itself. It can also be stuffed with other scraps.

65.

Placement of the wood, Peruvian money and other objects are tested for their relationship to one another and to the lines and shapes of the materials (Fig. 66).

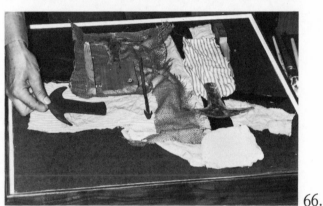

66.

Additional materials have been glued on and now the artist adds bold color with acrylic paints (Fig. 67). It takes about an hour for the layers of glue to dry hard. If you decide you don't like something where it is, you have time to remove it. When you work with acrylic paints you can quickly cover one color with another, should you change your thinking. You are not really committed to anything and there is a great deal of freedom.

67.

Here the artist places paint beneath some of the fabric edges so that color peeks through the loose weave of the fabrics (Fig. 68). Some of the bold pattern stripes are muted with paint. After the composition has completely dried, the entire surface is coated with an artists' glaze which draws the fabric to the backing, hardens, preserves and provides a subtle gloss. The polymer medium also makes the materials impervious to dust and deterioration.

(See the next page for the finished assemblage.)

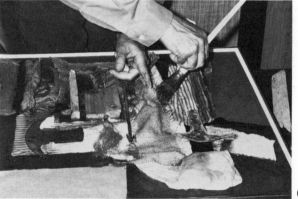

68.

69. PERUVIAN ARTISTRY, *Claude Bentley*

69.—The curved shapes of the money and the verticals and horizontals have been related and repeated in the different materials. The cloth cuff at right forms an uneven raised surface that both relates to and opposes the stiffer forms of the wood. Ragged and smooth edges, use of flat and wrinkled fabrics add to the visual and tactile excitement. Each raised portion catches light and shadow to give the work a constantly changing appearance.

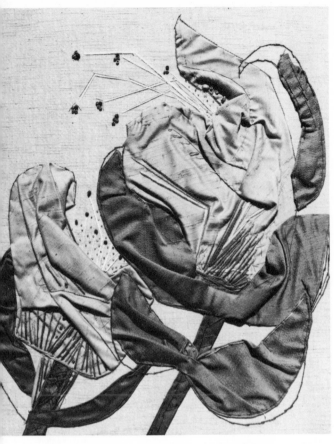

70. CANNAS, *Lee Snow*. Fabric scraps stitched to gold linen background. Red flowers of heavy silk, dark green leaves and stems. Beads are added for the flowers' stamens.

Photo: Helfant

71. ALPHABETICAL FUN, *Stephen Antonakos*. Wool and cotton fabrics machine stitched and glued. Wood and raised letters.

Courtesy, Miami Museum of Modern Art

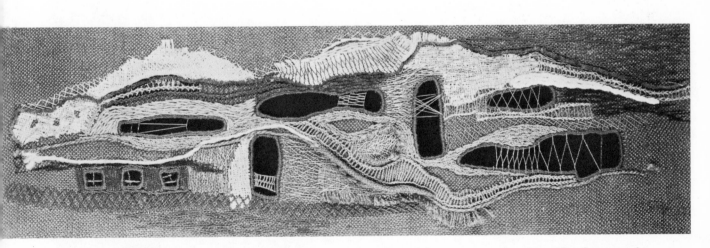

72. CACAO, *Evelyn Svec Ward*. Stitchery, appliqué and lace cut-work over a background of black velvet.

Courtesy of the artist

73. ST. VALENTINE'S DAY MASSACRE HOMAGE, *Bruce Conner and Errol Flynn.* Assorted feathers, net, glitter and glass.
Courtesy, San Francisco Museum of Art

74. KANSAS COLLAGE, *Enrique Riverón.*
Mementos and objects found in Kansas.
Photo: James Yarnell

75. POINT BETSY #2, *Nelson Howe*. Fabrics, dress patterns and paint.
Collection, The Chase Manhattan Bank, New York

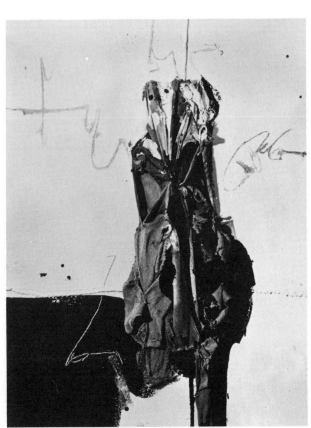

76. HOMÚNCULO, *Millares*. Burlap and paint.
Courtesy, Gallería Juana Mordó, Madrid

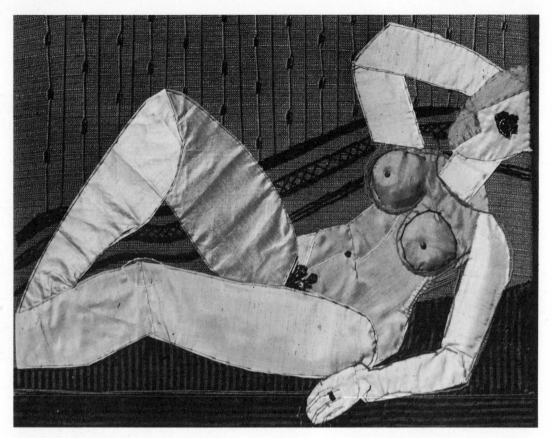

77. ODALISQUE, *Lee Snow*. The rich silk and satin fabrics lend themselves to the sensual subject matter.

    Courtesy of the artist

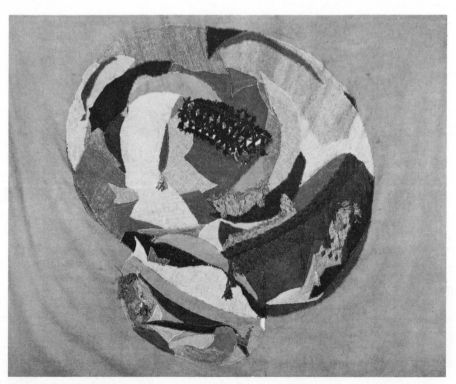

78. LLEU, *Dolores Elbert*. Handwoven cotton and wool fabrics in rich colors with decorative scraps of trim and tassels.

    Courtesy of the artist

79. WIND FIGURE, *Mark Friedman*. Fabric dipped in plaster and allowed to harden becomes a sculpture.
Courtesy, Sculptors Guild, Inc., New York

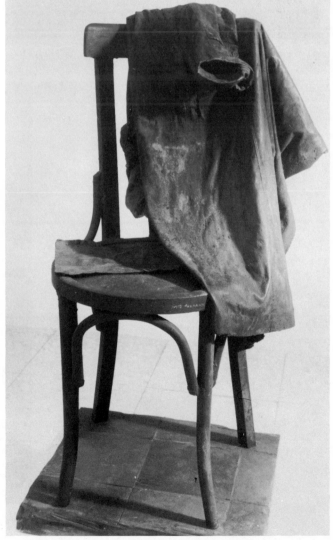

80. SILLA (CHAIR), *Julio L. Hernández*. Wood chair and slate hardened coat established as a sculpture attests to the artist's preoccupation with his environment.
Courtesy, Galería Juana Mordó, Madrid

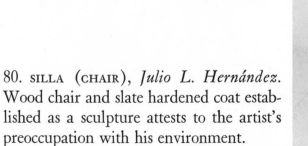

The examples on these pages are considered "soft sculptures."

81.—Soft forms, yet definite hard edges, are evident in this three-dimensional fabric composition.

82.—Stuffed high relief fabrics, glued and wrinkled materials, paint and wood chips are successfully employed.

81. STUFFED CLOTH FIGURE, *Sharyn Marshak*
Student, Deerfield High School

82. ABIGAIL, *Nancy Hahn*
Student, Deerfield High School

83.—Soft-sculptured fabric collage on a welded steel frame. The metal frame becomes a cradle for the cloth form and a strong unifying factor in the total fabric sculpture.

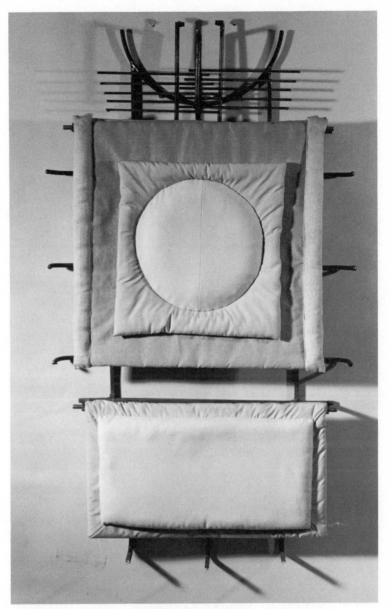

83. LUNAR FRAME, *Jeanne Boardman Knorr*
Collection, Mrs. Devorah Sherman, Winnetka, Illinois

84. STUFFED RUBBER GRUB, *Clayton Bailey*. Soft sculpture of latex and foam rubber.
Courtesy, The Art Institute of Chicago

85. PIER, *C. Robert Perrin*
Courtesy of the artist

85.—Scraps of wool, cotton, high- and low-pile carpeting are glued to a canvas background. The drawing is marked on the canvas, then the rug scraps cut to fit the shapes. The result is like a richly woven tapestry.

86.—Rug scraps combined with fabrics that are stitched and/or glued to the backing of loosely woven linen.

86. FLOWERS, *Hanna Silver*
Courtesy of the artist

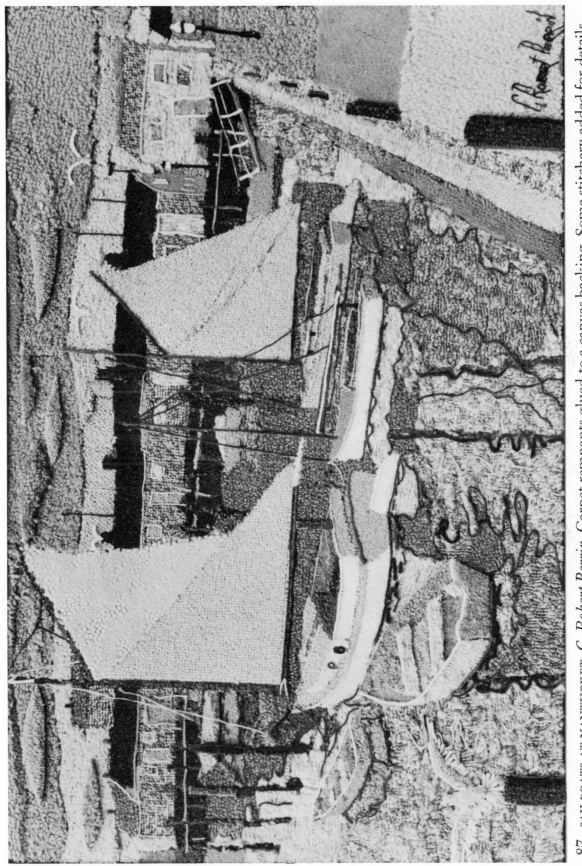

87. SAILBOATS AT NANTUCKET, *C. Robert Perrin.* Carpet remnants glued to a canvas backing. Some stitchery added for details. *Courtesy of the artist*

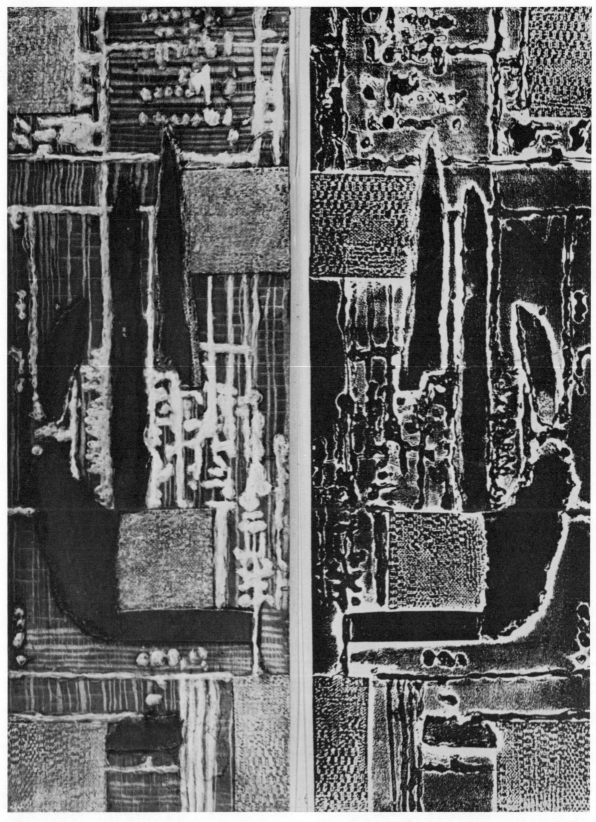

88. DESIGN NO. 5, *Nellie Deachman*. Swatches of textured wallpapers, dribbles of modeling paste and laminated pressboard comprise the plate's surface (left). Layers of the pressboard can be peeled off to produce nuances of greys and blacks, depending upon how the board is inked. The print (at right) is always the reverse image of the plate.

5 Collagraphs (Printmaking from Objects)

Printmaking is the process of placing ink on a raised surface and applying paper to that surface. The ink transfers to the paper and a print results. This is the principle of a date stamp on which raised numerals are inked and stamped to make an imprint on paper. A collagraph utilizes the same principle except that selected objects form the raised portions. Collagraphs can be made very simple for young children or more complex as one masters the technique of creating plates and prints.

Below, printmaker Evelyn Lewy demonstrates how to make a collagraph printing plate. She arranges and relates pieces of carefully selected miscellaneous scraps. The backing can be shirt cardboard, mat board or laminated pressboard. The raised areas will print solid black. The lower, uninked surfaces will remain white on the print. Sandpaper and other textured materials will look as rough as they feel when they are printed. The objects must be glued solidly to the backing with a waterproof all-purpose cement. The plate should be sprayed with artists' glaze or lacquer to preserve it and enable you to remove the ink with benzine after prints are pulled.

89. Making a collagraph printing plate

46

90.

91.

92.

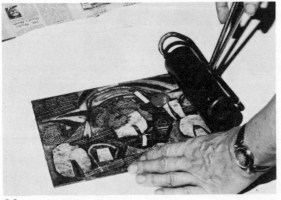

93.

The following pictures demonstrate the printing of a plate.

Lightly dampened paper should be used when hand printing from a collage plate (Fig. 90). Japanese Hosho paper or specially prepared wood block papers are best. The paper is dampened by placing it, sized, glossy side up, between two blotters that have been moistened with a sponge (Fig. 91). Then wrap the blotters in heavy plastic such as an old shower curtain and allow to set overnight. Do not put paper directly under a stream of water or it will tear apart.

When you are ready to print, place either oil-base or water-base printer's ink on a slab of glass or an enamel pan (Fig. 92). Roll out the ink with a printer's brayer until it is smoothly distributed on the roller.

Roll the inked brayer over the printing plate until it appears to have an even layer of ink on all the raised (relief) surfaces (Fig. 93).

Remove the paper from between the blotters and place it *sized side down* on the plate, leaving about an inch margin around the plate (Fig. 94). With your hands, press the paper onto the plate, molding it around the edges of the plate and into the grooves of the design. Rub gently into the edges and the texture with your fingers. Be careful not to move the paper on the plate or a blurred image will result.

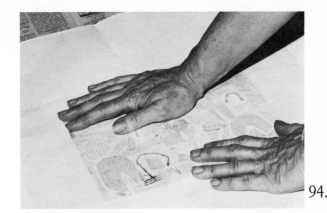

94.

Then pass a clean, hard rubber brayer back and forth over the paper, exerting as much pressure as you can without causing the paper to wrinkle (Fig. 95). Soon the design will come through.

95.

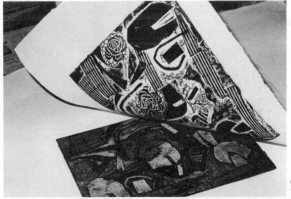

96.

When you think the ink has transferred to the paper, peel the paper from the plate (Fig. 96).

97. UNTITLED, *Evelyn Lewy*. The finished print (left) and the inked plate (right). Observe how the different shapes and materials printed. The plate is composed of a lace doily, corrugated cardboard, pipe cleaners, needle threader, silver foil and scraps of textured wallpapers.

98. LIFE II, *Evelyn Lewy*. Plate and print

98.—Plate, at left, contains coins, decorative sequins, hair comb, zinc printing plate, wallpapers, fabric, corrugated cardboard, pieces of a strawberry carton, cloth army insignia. Print, at right, was made on a press, but it could be hand printed as in the demonstration on pages 46 and 47.

99. RUINS OF ITALY, *Margaret Perlman*. Plate   100. Print

99. & 100.—Cardboard, fabrics and wallpapers form the relief surfaces. Magazine illustrations of columns and ancient buildings are pasted on the pressboard backing. The illustrations are cut into so that the columns will become raised and the negative areas will be white. The plate is at the left; the print at the right.

101. LIFE III (STATE I), *Evelyn Lewy.* Plate

102. Proof

101.—Backs of plastic tiles become the plate for assorted objects. This is the beginning of a print plate that will eventually have many more forms and textures within each square. The artist has pulled a proof (Fig. 102) to observe how the shapes relate and to help her decide what more has to be added.

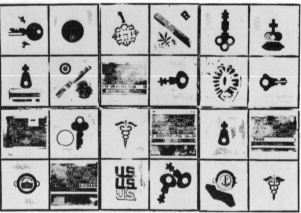

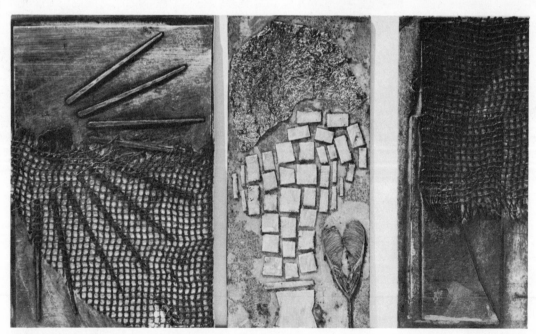

103. Printing plates made by young children consist of raised surfaces made from loosely woven fabrics, toothpicks, crushed aluminum foil, seed pods and cardboard shapes. Evelyn Lewy, Instructor.

104. UNTITLED, *James Warren Felter*. Plate

105. Print

104.—Water putty mixed with white glue forms the Aztec symbols that are repeated by impressing authentic designs from beads into the soft putty. Silver foil, embossed cardboard, string and walnut shavings are used for this enriched surface plate. The plate is covered with lacquer as a preservative; then printed (Fig. 105).

106. THE ODD COUPLE, *Jacqueline Fogel*
   Photo: Rupert Finegold

6 Working with Wood

Wood is a favorite material for constructions and assemblages because of its unlimited supply and variety of shapes and textures. In preference to new lumber, artists seek wood that is weathered and rubbed smooth by the seas or the winds, wood that is broken and charred into tortured forms and wood scraps of every kind. Planks and pieces of two-by-four's, decorative turnings from furniture, driftwood, dried branches and roots found in forests yield an exciting array of pieces that can be used by themselves or in combination with other materials.

Wood is a living, breathing material. Old wood, weather-beaten, gray and roughened, seems to whisper its history; maybe once part of a great tree and now reduced to the sad fragment of an old rocking chair, a child's toy or a dried, dead branch. But its usefulness is not yet over, because the artist finds in it a function that attests to its durability and aesthetic qualities.

Wood may be assembled in many ways. Small scraps may be fastened to a backing or to one another with glues, nails, corrugated fasteners or screws. Lathed turnings such as furniture legs and spindles can be assembled by drilling holes in the pieces

106.—Old furniture legs, spindles and other pieces of shaped wood are assembled into a delightful sculpture. Doorknobs and drawer handles are used for many of the details. Pieces are pegged with dowels and glued together, then carved and painted.

and gluing short lengths of dowel rods into them to hold them together.

Adhesives for woods are contact cement, plastic resins, white glue and epoxy glues. Consult the glue chart on page 119, keeping in mind that you will need a waterproof glue if the sculpture is to be used out of doors.

To secure glued wood joints, you may have to devise your own clamps. You can use "C" clamps or miter clamps, which are available in hardware stores in many sizes. Large and irregular shapes often require invention. Strips from rubber innertubes can be stretched and crisscrossed. Bricks or other heavy objects may be placed on top of glued pieces to hold them down. Rubber bands and clothespins will clamp together small forms while the glue sets.

Holes and cracks in wood may be filled with wood putty or plastic wood. Simple carpentry can be accomplished with hand saws, hammers, chisels and screwdrivers. Power saws, drills and sanders expedite the work.

Some artists like to rub in oil color to give the wood a special effect or highlight. To do this, dip a rag in paint and simply rub the color where it is needed. Often, old wood serves as an interesting canvas for a painted figure.

Wood that has been lying about for many years may have some insect larvae in it. So it's a good idea to wash the wood with warm water and a firm brush. (Don't use soaps or detergents; they add chemicals to

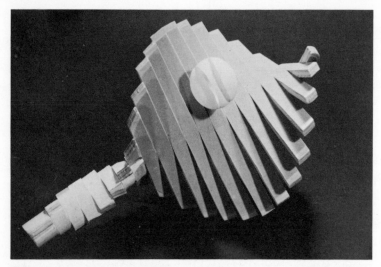

107. A ping-pong paddle and ball

108. Wooden salad bowls

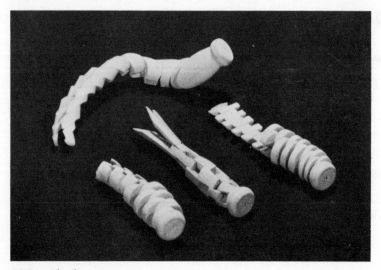

109. Clothespins

the wood.) Some artists spray wood with insecticides, but others maintain that this changes the ability of the wood to retain paints. It's a matter of deciding how you, personally, prefer to work with the material.

However you decide to arrange the pieces of wood you select, you will discover new patterns, textures and relationships of wood to itself and to other objects.

Fragmenting Forms

An exercise in finding a new relationship to the parts of a given form is to fragment or cut an object into smaller parts and explore the many different possible shapes it may take. In the examples on this page, each object was fragmented by cutting on a band saw. Then the parts were glued together in a new arrangement. All examples, Institute of Design, I.I.T., Ray Pearson, Instructor.

Painting on Wood

Weathered wood or other pieces of found wood that have texture and tone can be worked into a composition, and may be painted in addition, to enhance the work. The artist may use oils, acrylics or temperas, depending upon his own preference. Most oil paints (those that come in tubes or large paint cans) may be used out of doors and will last for several years. On this page are two examples of painting on wood.

110. SPOOL END, *Larry Koetz.* An old barrel top has circular forms repeated in the painting with repeated holes drilled through.
Student, Deerfield High School

111. CAT, *Siol.* Oil painting on block of found, weathered wood.

On the following several pages are examples of the tremendous variety of uses for wood in art.

112. WOOD SCULPTURE. Scraps of wood from industrial design classes, brought to the art department, are assembled into wildly imaginative sculptures.
Student, Skiles Jr. High

113. CONSTRUCTION, *Maury Killey*. Wood scraps and slivers.
Student, Niles West High School

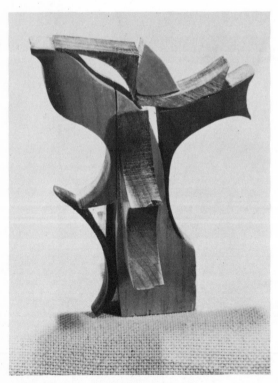

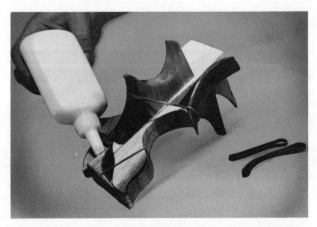

114. & 115. SCRAP CONSTRUCTION. Devising methods for clamping together odd-shaped pieces of wood is as great a challenge as assembling the forms. Rubber bands, strategically placed after gluing (right), worked well for this sculpture.
Student, Skiles Jr. High

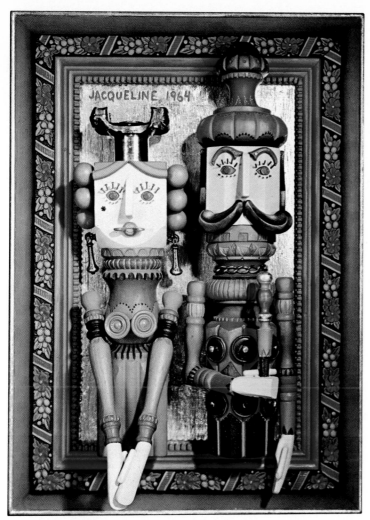

A ROYAL PORTRAIT, *Jacqueline Fogel.* Furniture parts, wood trim, paint
Photo: Rupert Finegold

BODY FACTORY, *Ralph Arnold.* Wood, metal gears, paper
Photo: Dona Meilach

CHAINED TO TIME, *Elvie Ten Hoor.* Clock parts, chain, paper, paint *Collection, Dr. and Mrs. Melvin Meilach*
Photo: Dona Meilach

MEET MISS SUBWAY, *Jacqueline Fogel.* Furniture parts, wood trim, paint
Photo: Rupert Finegold
Courtesy, Krasner Gallery, New York

117. ORGANIC ORDER, *Lester Rebbeck*

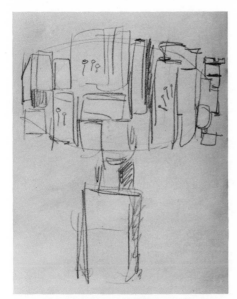

116. Sketch for sculpture 117.

117.—Scrap pieces of wood, assembled with screws that become part of the design, are developed according to a pre-planned sketch (Fig. 116).

118.—Weathered wood has repeated round shapes. Milk pods, pegs and holes, and roofing nails are carefully arranged so the sculpture is interesting on all sides.

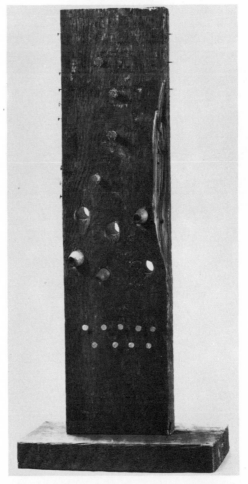

118. GARDEN STELE, *Lester Rebbeck*
Collection, Dr. and Mrs. Meilach

58

119. UNTITLED, *Robert Pierron*. A section from a table pedestal, wood spindles, paint brush handles and a wood potato masher.

120. LET THERE BE MUSIC, *Robert Borchard*. Scrap wood glued to a wood board. Nails purposely protrude to create another dimension and repeat design.

Collection, Lester Rebbeck, Arlington Heights, Illinois

121. DOWEL PUSSYWILLOWS, *Gail Barazini Student, N. I. S. C., Chicago*

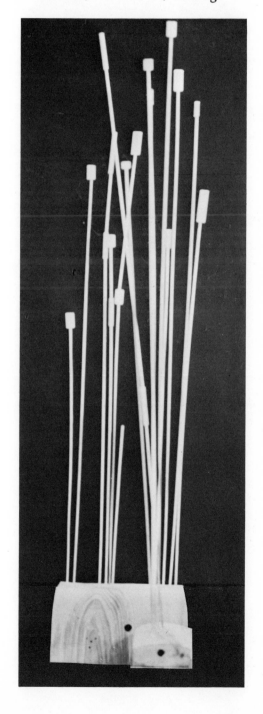

122. UNTITLED, *Gordon Wagner.* Driftwood, smoothed by the ocean, assembled and painted.
Courtesy of the artist

123. LE MARSEILLAISE, *Robert Mallary*. Plywood, billboard tearings, polyester, welded steel.
Collection, Mr. and Mrs. Arnold Maremont, Winnetka, Illinois

124. UNTITLED, *Robert Borchard Collection, Charles Brockman, Arlington Heights, Illinois*

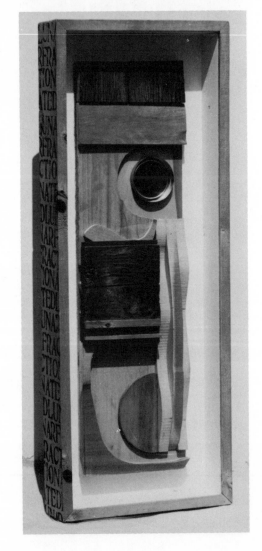

124.—Parts of wood crate with stamped letters and glass became the frame for assembled shapes of wood and a can cover.

125. PARADE, *John Little*. Wood, leather and wire on masonite.
   Courtesy of the artist

126. RAINBOW GIRLS IN MIRROR, *James Russell.* Construction of wood with paint added.
Courtesy, Ruth White Gallery, New York

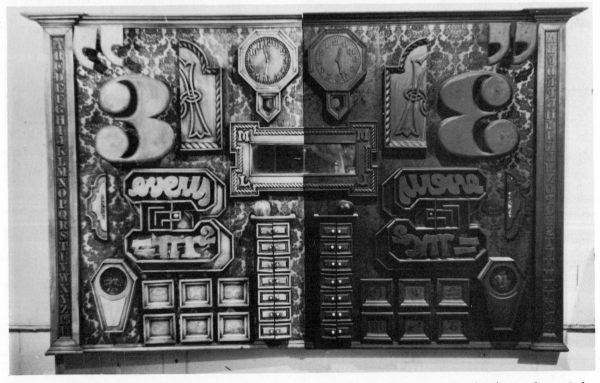

127. STUDY ROOM, *James Russell.* Construction with wood. Items are duplicated on right
side to form the reverse image.
Courtesy, Ruth White Gallery, New York

129. THE FAMILY THAT BOWLS TOGETHER STAYS TO-
GETHER, *Robert Pierron*. Laminated bowling pins.
One pin was split and the slice reshaped with facial
features, then reassembled.

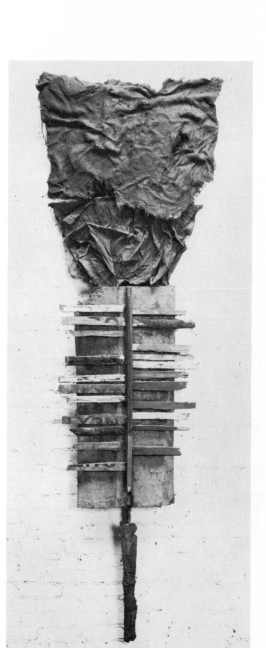

128. THE GENERAL, *Robert Mallary*. Wood,
polyester.and rags.
Courtesy, Allan Stone Gallery, New York

130. FOOT, *Betty Parsons*. Weathered wood, painted.
Courtesy, Grand Central Moderns, New York

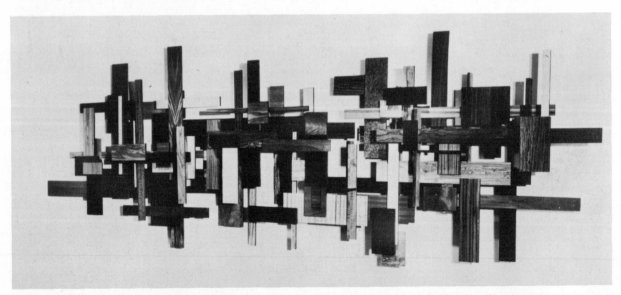

131. WALL SCULPTURE, *William Bowie*. Made from 150 types of plywood veneers.
Collection, U. S. Plywood Co., New York

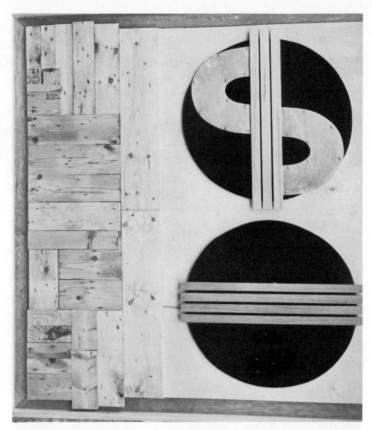

132. CONSTRUCTION IN WOOD AND METAL,
Michael Rothenstein
   Courtesy, Hamilton Galleries Ltd., London

133. CABINET, *James Russell*. Wood miscellany within
a wooden cabinet catches interesting shadows.
   Courtesy, Ruth White Gallery, New York

134. BEAUTY PARLOR, *Jacqueline Fogel*. Wooden spindles, legs, parts from cabinets, knobs, and an astonishing variety of decorative items from old furniture.
  Photo: Rupert Finegold

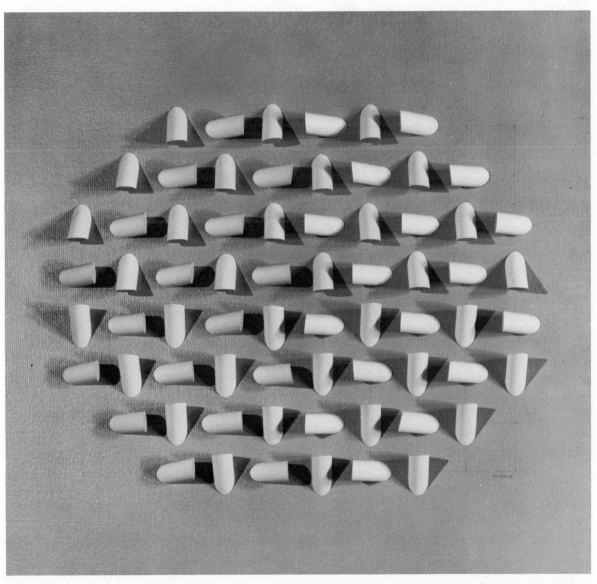

135. UNTITLED, *James McNair*. Wood dowels shaped and glued to a backing in a geometrical arrangement.
Collection, The Chase Manhattan Bank, New York

136. THE ROSE, *Jacob Burck*. Steel pipes, trowels
and scraps welded together and arranged in a
bronze vase.

Courtesy, Conrad Gallery, Chicago

7　Metal Assemblage

For the artist who works with the materials of his environment, it is only natural that things mechanical should appear in his art. The artist is living in the machine age; he is a product of it. Whether the final piece of art depicts a mechanical image or uses the mechanical item to depict another image, it amply illustrates the artist's ability to transform the everyday things he sees about him.

For the artist, a junkyard filled with mechanical flotsam is an exercise in mental stimulation. He scrounges for automobile parts, pipes, pieces of worn tools, clock parts, farm machinery—anything of interesting shape that might form a vital relationship with other items or make a pleasing design.

Once the artist decides on the objects he will use, his next problem is technical. How will he join the conglomeration to give it new life?

Depending upon the object and its shape, it may be joined by bolting, screwing, slotting one piece and sliding another piece into it or by folding it within another piece of thin metal. Gluing is a possibility too. Often the specially compounded epoxy glues will adhere one metal object to another. Epoxies are so strong they have taken the place of riveting in many airplane assemblies. Metals can also be joined by heat in the welding and soldering techniques.

When metals are joined by bolting, screwing and gluing, the joined parts are still two separate entities that can be broken apart. When heat fuses metals, as in soldering and welding, the molecules of the materials are actually broken down and they flow into one another or into the metal agents used with heat, such as solder or a welding rod. This molecular transformation creates the most permanent joint. To solder and weld, some technical knowledge about the characteristics of metal is required.

Soldering is a comparatively low-heat technique used with thin metals such as brass, copper and bronze. A soldered joint is often stronger than the base metal. In soft soldering the joining agent is lead or tin solder that has a melting point between 400° and 700° Fahrenheit. Hard soldering requires a silver solder that melts at temperatures ranging from 1160° to 1500°. In this technique, the solder fills a space between the two pieces of metal to be joined, adhering them to one another in a permanent bond. An electric soldering iron, soldering gun or an air-acetylene torch may be used for soft soldering. Hard soldering for thin metals requires any kind of portable air-gas unit, such as a propane torch.

Welding with oxyacetylene is required for heavier metals such as iron, steel, large, thick pieces of bronze, copper, aluminum and brass. The welding technique itself is simple and easy enough to learn in one class session. For people who wish to tackle more complicated welding jobs, an understanding of the technical aspects of the materials and tools will be essential. This involves a working knowledge of metals and alloys, ferrous and nonferrous metals and the welding rods required for joining unlike materials. Even this is not too complex. Many high school art classrooms include welding equipment, and the students turn out excellent art work from every conceivable kind of metal or metal object.

Each of the sculptures illustrated here should be studied carefully to appreciate how deftly and ingeniously the artist trans-forms a recognizable object into a new relationship in which its original use may be almost completely obscured. In its new relationship it may imply something totally different, or even abstract—speed, mechanization, humor, organic and sensual images. The forms may be solid in the space they occupy, or they may be light and airy, allowing space to flow in and out among the shapes and become part of the sculpture.

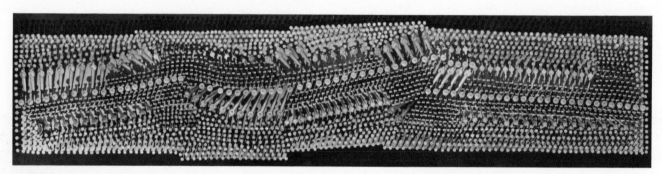

137. VERTEBRATE CONFIGURATION, *David Partridge*
Courtesy of the Director of the Tate Gallery, London

138.—Tin cans and tin-can parts assembled with liquid solder. Hairclips are bent and attached for feet and legs.

138. MOUSE

139.—The elephant's trunk and legs, made from bottle caps, are strung on wires. The caps closest to the tin-can body were liquid-soldered together and then to the cans. The wire trunk can be moved in various directions.

Examples 138. and 139. by eighth grade students, Woodlawn Jr. High School, Baltimore County, Baltimore, Md., T. R. Pokorny, Instructor.

139. ELEPHANT

Epoxy cements will hold almost any metals. Read the directions before using and take care to select the correct material for the given problem. Epoxy materials are called glues, cements and compounds. Manufacturers claim that many epoxy joints will withstand stresses up to a ton after hardening.

140.—Epoxy compounds come in two tubes that must be mixed; one is epoxy resin, the other is hardener. Combine the two epoxy components just before using. Place equal amounts from each tube on a surface.

140.

141.—Mix them together until they reach the consistency recommended in the directions. Make small batches that can be used within twenty to thirty minutes after mixing. Use in temperatures no colder than 60°.

141.

142.—Immediately after epoxy is mixed, spread it on both the surfaces to be joined. (Surfaces should always be clean and free from foreign particles.) Then press the glued surfaces together and do not move them until they are dry. Clamping may be needed for some joints. Epoxies can be removed from the skin with nail polish remover or denatured alcohol.

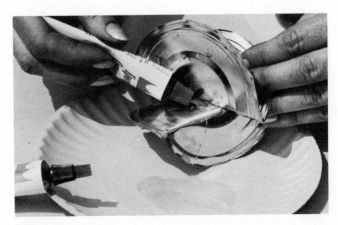

142.

143.

Soldering

143.—Materials for soldering include a wire brush, steel wool or emery paper for cleaning the metal, soldering flux, which comes in liquid or paste, solder (lead, tin, or resin core) and a soldering iron or gun.

144.

144.—The metals to be soldered should be clean and roughened with an abrasive steel wool or emery cloth. Only lightweight metals such as copper, brass, silver, steel and tin should be soldered. Heavy metals are not successfully soldered.

145.

145.—Flux should be applied liberally to the areas to be joined.

146.—To solder, allow the iron to heat up. Dip the hot point into the flux; then apply some solder to the fluxed area on the metal until the solder melts and begins to flow. Move the solder and iron along the edges to be joined until the solder flows. It hardens as it cools. After the joint has cooled, wash off the flux with a solution of vinegar and water. When joining a thick and a thin piece of metal, the thicker portion requires more heat.

146.

The following examples have some soldered parts.

147. FEMME FATALE, *Robert Pierron*

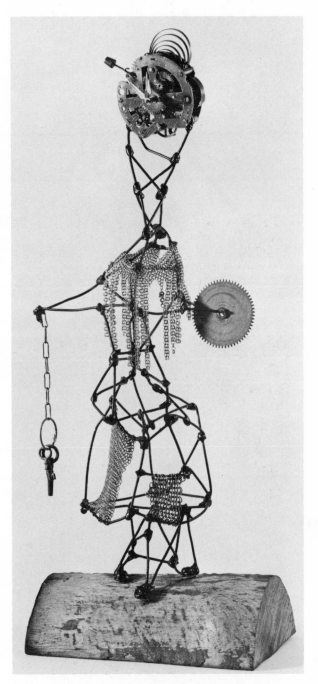

147.—Sterling silverware and hollow-ware parts on driftwood fragments are set in two small boxes mounted on the cover from a silverware chest. Some soldering; mostly glued.

148.—The artist has fashioned an intricate wire skeleton with chains, keys and a working clock that can be wound and set in motion.

148. PORTRAIT OF GRANDMOTHER NO. 2, *William Accorsi*
Courtesy, Dene Ulin, Agent
Collection, Lorna Opatow, New York

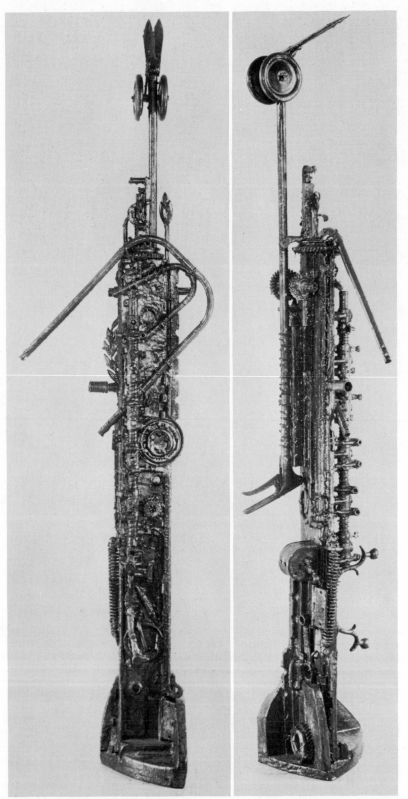

150. TOWER OF BABEL, *Arthur Secunda.* Nine-foot-high scrap metal assemblage.
Courtesy, Fleischer Anhalt Gallery, Los Angeles
Collection, The University of Uppsala, Sweden.

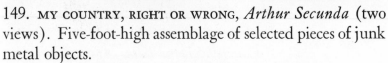

149. MY COUNTRY, RIGHT OR WRONG, *Arthur Secunda* (two views). Five-foot-high assemblage of selected pieces of junk metal objects.

Courtesy, Fleischer Anhalt Gallery, Los Angeles
Collection, The Moderna Museet, Stockholm

151. CIGAR MAKER'S FAMILY, *Robert Pierron*. Humor and wit are combined with ingenuity and craftsmanship. The family, composed of pieces of sterling silverware, inhabit an antique wooden cigar-mold box.

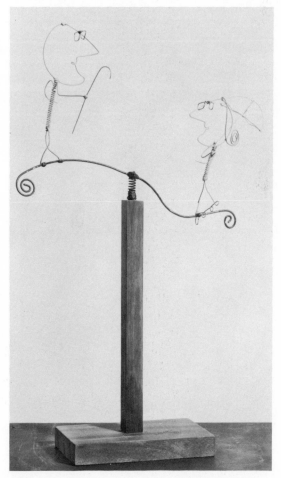

152. BALANCING ACT, *William Accorsi*. Wire and springs.
Courtesy, Ontario East Gallery, Chicago

153. SUNDAY IN CENTRAL PARK, *William Accorsi*. Wire and springs.
Courtesy, Ontario East Gallery, Chicago

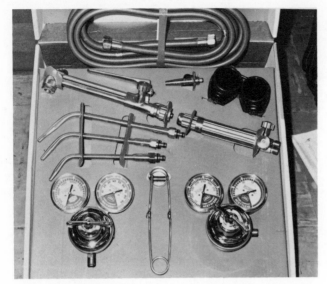

154. Welding kit

Welding

Anyone who wishes to work directly with metals may begin by using a small propane torch, but eventually a welder's kit may be desired. Only a small working area is actually required and this space should be shielded with an inflammable asbestos board to keep sparks from igniting other objects. Welding equipment may be purchased piece by piece. A complete welding kit consists of a torch handle, various sized torch tips, goggles, an igniter, pressure regulators, cutting attachments and hoses (Fig. 154).

Detailed instructions for using the torch and for welding come with the kit and are available from a welders' supply house. A kit does *not* contain the gas tanks.

155.—Oxygen and acetylene tanks with pressure regulators attached. Tanks may be rented. When the gas is used up, the dealer replaces the empty tank with a full tank.

156.—A special cutting tip enables you to cut metal quickly with the heat of the torch.

155. Oxygen and acetylene tanks

156. Cutting tip

157.—The welder's torch with a tip attached, a welding rod (which is melted to form the bridge between the objects to be welded), pliers, and hinge to which nails have been affixed.

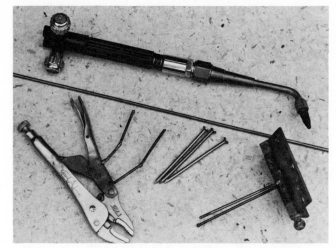

157.

158.—Close-up showing how the welding rod flows onto the nails to congeal the mass together in a permanent fusion.

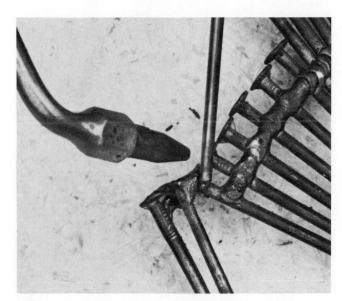

158.

159.—The welding rod may also be used to supply metal where needed, such as for the details of eyes, nose and mouth.

159.

160. DON QUIXOTE AND SANCHO PANZA, *from Spain, artist unknown*. Welded nails. *Collection, Dr. and Mrs. Melvin Meilach*

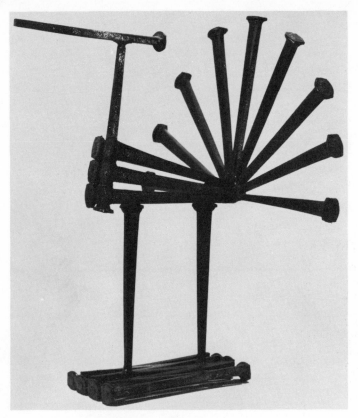

161. PEACOCK, *Robert Pierron*. Large spikes form the body, legs, feathers and base.

162. BUGHOUSE SQUARE, *Jacob Burck*. Railroad spikes are cleverly transformed to symbolize an audience listening to a speaker.

Courtesy, The Conrad Gallery, Chicago

163. BATS, *Jacob Burck*. Welded hinges.
Courtesy, The Conrad Gallery, Chicago

164. PIRANHA, *Jacob Burck*. Pliers with saws added for fins and weed diggers for tails mounted on welding rods. Front fins are from expansion shields.
Courtesy, The Conrad Gallery, Chicago

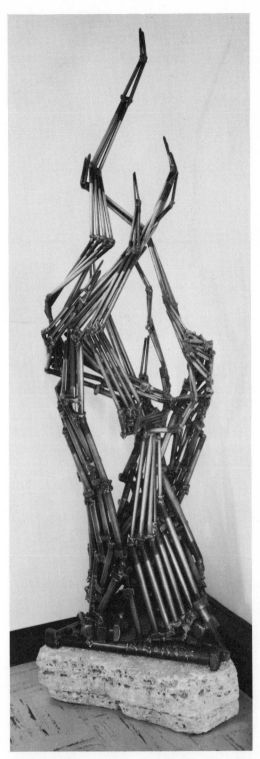

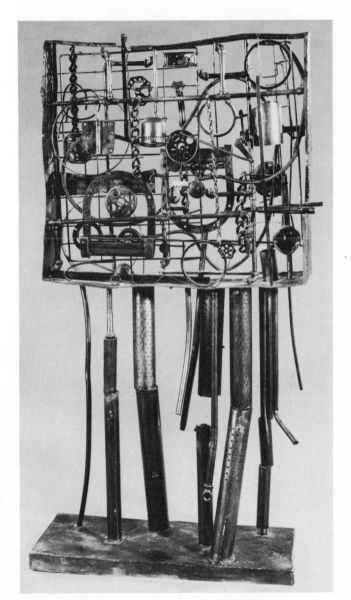

165. THE BURNING BUSH, *Egon Weiner*. Steel bolts and nuts in a welded assembly.
Courtesy of the artist

166. ANALOGY, *David Gray*. Welded steel objects.
Collection, The Walker Art Center, Minneapolis

167. YOUNG BOSWELL, *Jacob Burck*. Iron parts from an old waterpump. Springs form the hair and an old flat iron becomes Boswell's tricornered hat.

Courtesy, The Conrad Gallery, Chicago

168. REGAL GROUP, *Helen Stoller*. Bolts, nuts, chisel blade and machined parts.

Courtesy, Ruth White Gallery, New York

169. THE WORLD OF MOHAMMED, *Friede-rich Werthmann*
   Courtesy of the artist

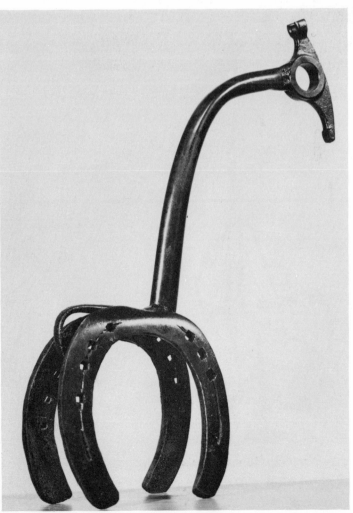

170. GIRAFFE, *Sergio Lanzavecchia*
Courtesy, Galleria L'88, Rome

With metal you can get widely different effects. Metal sculptures can convey a whole range of feelings, from solid and ponderous to light and delicate.

171. HORSES, *Jacob Burck*. Hooks, pulley parts, spikes and miscellany. Here steel has the look of light line drawings.

Courtesy, The Conrad Gallery, Chicago

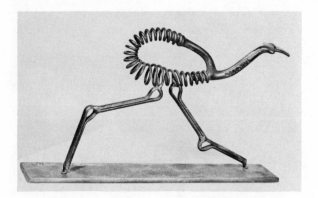

172. RUNNING OSTRICH, *Jacob Burck*. Lifter from an old-fashioned stove and large cotter pins become a form that suggests grace.

Courtesy, The Conrad Gallery, Chicago

173. SNOB, *Sergio Lanzavecchia*. Chains, keys, rake and plow parts, drain grates.

Courtesy, Galleria L'88, Rome

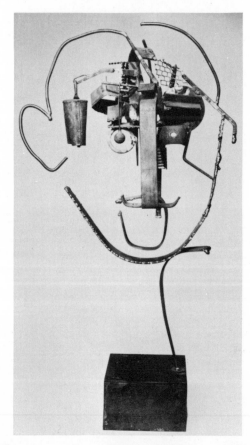

174. HEAD SCULPTURE, *William Bowie*. Steel parts with bronze accents.

Courtesy, The Sculpture Studio, Inc.

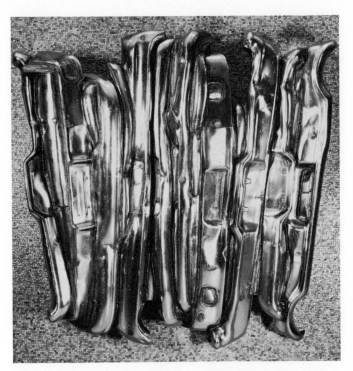

176. TRIPTYCH, *Jason Seley*. Welded steel bumpers. *Collection, The Chase Manhattan Bank*

175. JOAN OF PARK, *John Kearney*. Welded steel chromium automobile bumpers.

Collection, Dr. E. Schwartz, Flossmoor, Illinois

177. SWINGING OUT, *Jason Seley*. Welded steel. A basic shape is repeated in this open sculpture.

Collection, The Chase Manhattan Bank, New York

178. ACCUMULATION OF TEAPOTS, *Arman*. Certain manufactured items will catch an artist's attention and he will assemble them for their shape, their surface reflections and patterns.

Courtesy, Galerie Ileana Sonnabend, Paris

179. ACCUMULATION OF TEAPOTS, II, *Arman*. Teapots cut in half and assembled within a plexiglass box.

Collection, Walker Art Center, Minneapolis

180. FAMILY GROUP, *Egon Weiner*. The metal form remaining after shapes have been cut out of it can suggest an identity. This form was picked up among castoff metals. No additional work was provided by the sculptor.

181. SHIP, *Egon Weiner*. Rusted bolts protruding from an iron bar suggest the boat form. Once given identity by the artist's imagination, the found object is forever a sculpture.

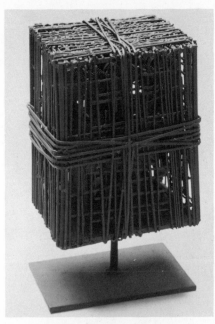

182. PRISONER, *Walter Yarwood*. Gears within a welded steel cage.
  Collection, Art Gallery of Ontario, Canada

183. THE REAPER, *Oliver Andrews*
  Collection, Los Angeles County Museum

184. ODYSSEY, *John LaFarge*
  Courtesy, The Betty Parsons Gallery, New York

185. MARTIAL, *Enrique Riverón*
  Photo: Sidney Tal-Mason
  Courtesy of the artist

ESCAPING HEAD, *Alfonso Ossorio*. Mixed media, including glass
eyes, marble, driftwood
Collection, Anthony Bower, New York

EGO DÑs #1, *Alfonso Ossorio*. Mixed media

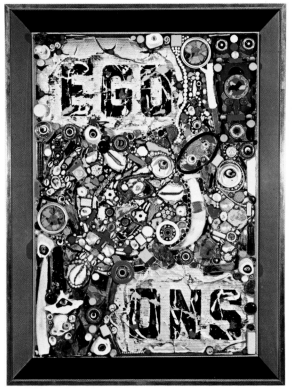

THE MARINE WORKS, *Robert Indiana*. Weathered wood, nails,
bolts, wheels, paint
Collection, The Chase Manhattan Bank, New York

186. THE CITY, *Arthur Secunda.* Metal assemblage.
Courtesy, Fleischer Anhalt Gallery, Los Angeles
State Collection, Sweden

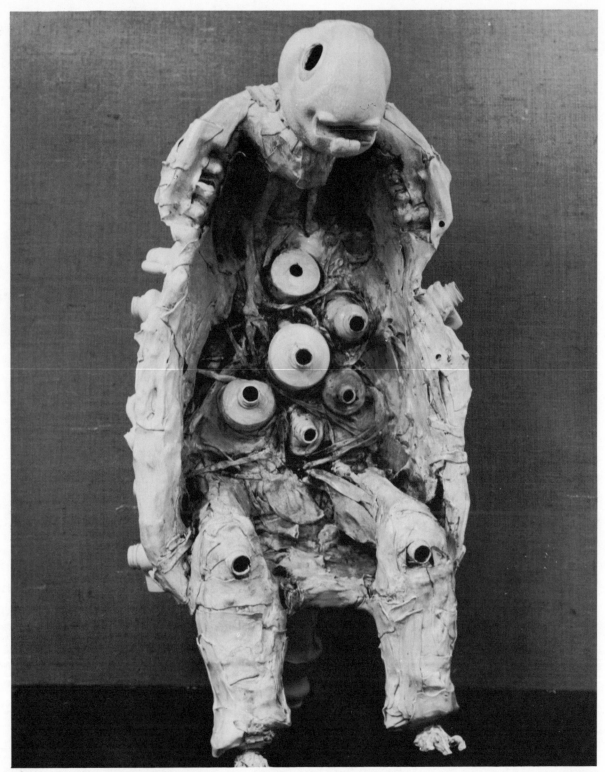

187. MOCK TURTLE, *David Huntley*. Created from plastic bottles and toys, transformed by heating, gluing and coating with acrylic gesso.
   Courtesy of the artist

8 Plastics

Plastic as an art form is still in the experimental stage. This new material, borrowed from industry, is stimulating artists to explore the nature and potential of the many forms of plastic available. Polymer emulsions and white glue, which is a polyvinyl resin (liquid plastic product), that adhere, glaze and harden, and acrylic paints, have been covered in previous chapters. But there are more than twenty varieties of plastics, ranging from soft transparent sandwich bags to hard plexiglass. All may be employed for art.

The techniques shown here illustrate the use of plastic objects found around the kitchen, playroom and laundry room. Polyethylene containers used for soaps and bleaches may be transformed into an endless variety of statements by the artist. Children may simply decorate detergent bottles by gluing other objects to them. The material itself may be employed as a modeling material, as demonstrated by David Huntley. Sharp knives, glue, plastic putty and low heat can quickly alter the shape and function of plastic.

Styrene and plastic foams can be directly sculpted and assembled. The sculptor may carve these materials and use them as a mold, a technique which has been adapted to large concrete slabs for decorative building facades.

The growing variety of available plastic materials still has to be explored beyond mere technical handling. They have limitations as well as potentials. Through innovation, trial and error, the artist discovers the expressive potential of plastic as a material with unique qualities.

188.—Plastic body parts from old dolls are used whole and fragmented to create an unusual relief construction. Plastic parts required a plastic putty to adhere them. For rubber, a vulcanizing compound was used at room temperature.

188. *Courtesy, David Huntley*

In these pictures, David Huntley demonstrates an assembly of plastic and rubber parts.

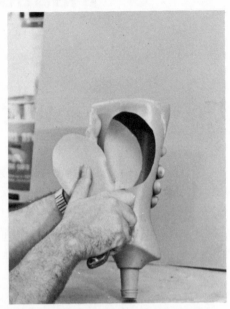

189. A detergent bottle is cut with a sharp knife.

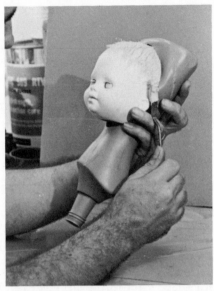

190. A plastic doll's head is put into the hole, using an epoxy filler similar in consistency and use to a soft putty. It hardens with exposure to the air after half an hour.

191. Doll's arms are attached with filler to the figure built up from plastic toy parts, laundry detergent bottles and rubber balls.

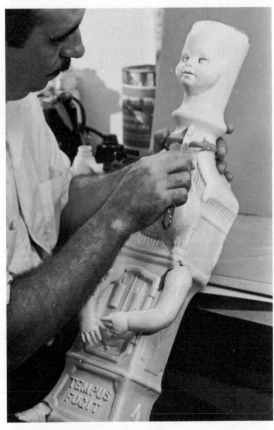

192. The entire piece is coated with acrylic gesso.

Photo series courtesy David Huntley

193. TEMPUS FUGIT, *David Huntley*. Each discarded plastic item has a new relationship and meaning in the context of the new figure.

194. Polyethylene plastic can be easily assembled by a welding technique. Materials consist of strips of the polyethylene culled from detergent and bleach bottles. A mat board knife is best for cutting the strips.

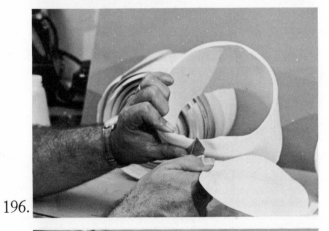

195. Slice off the top of the bottle; you will be using the body of the bottle to create the strips.

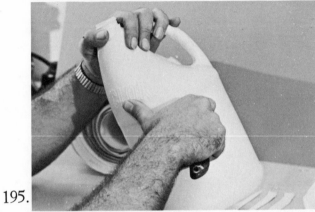

196. Cut off the bottom, leaving the tube of the body.

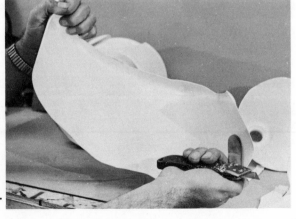

197. Make a vertical cut down the bottle so that it will be a flat piece.

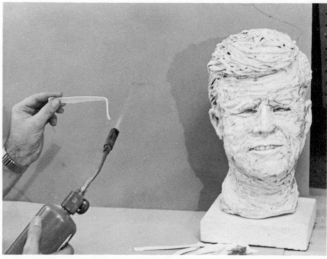

198. Then begin to cut strips from the bottles. (Note how the curved bodies of the bottles at the back of the table have been prepared for strip cutting.)

199. Each strip is softened by heat until it becomes amorphous enough to fuse with another softened piece. A propane torch, available in most hardware stores, is an adequate heat source. (Extra propane gas cartridges are also available.) An oxygen-acetylene welding unit produces too hot a heat. The heat from a gas stove could be used, but you would have difficulty controlling the temperature.

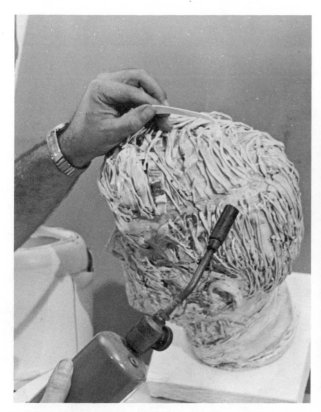

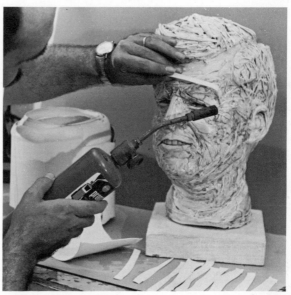

200. This head of John F. Kennedy was built up completely from such strips. The armature is an old football helmet with an empty plastic bottle jammed into the helmet for a base.

201. The result is a rough-textured, highly tactile sculpture.

All photos courtesy of the artist

202. EURYNOME AND OPHION, *David Huntley*. Polyethylene with a steel frame.

Two techniques used in this sculpture are shown below.

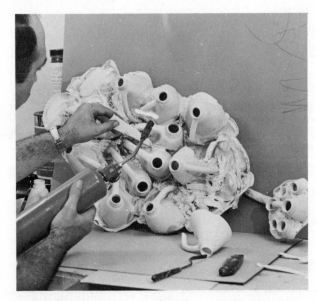

203. Leftover plastic bottle tops are combined with strips in the softening technique shown on the previous pages.

204. Some epoxy seal may be combined with the welding.

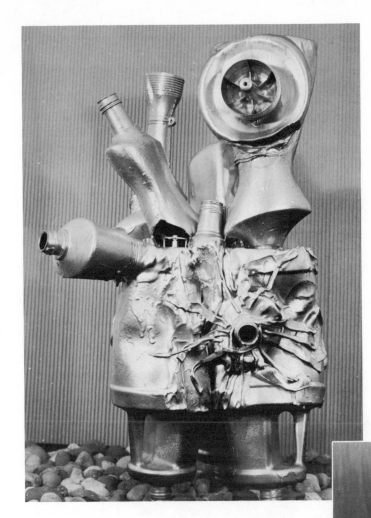

205. URANUS, *David Huntley.* In combination with the original bottle forms, any number of effects can be achieved by constructing plastic strips into other shapes.

206. MNEMOSYNE, *David Huntley.* Polyethylene.

All photos courtesy of the artist

207. RHINOCEROTID, *David Huntley*. Polyethylene bottles, caps, packing parts, balls and strips are painted a metallic color and simulate the effect of a metal sculpture.

208. ARGES, *David Huntley* (two views). Polyethylene parts, welded, conform to all the requirements of sculpture.

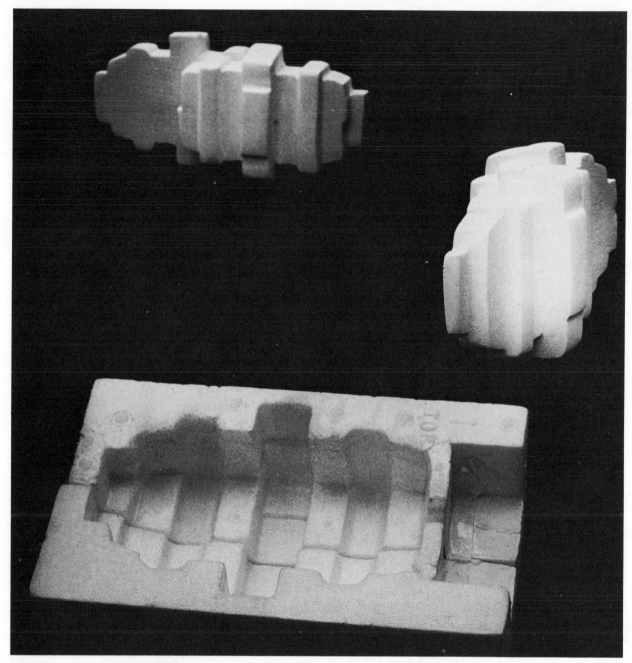

209. PLASTIC CONSTRUCTIONS, *Tom Harris*. Many products in the plastics family can be adapted to art projects. Here styrene, often used for packing and decorative objects, has been given another identity. The shapes are cut from a rectangular form (foreground), then assembled with white glue.

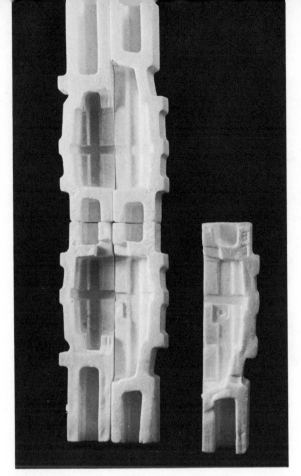

Often the shapes within the forms of styrene packing materials can be assembled into attractive sculptures that catch the changing light in dramatic ways. Moving shadows can give the whole sculpture different forms and shapes. This material may be cut with a sharp knife or with a sharp, heated blade.

210. STRUCTURE, *Tom Harris*. These negative shapes once held a television set.

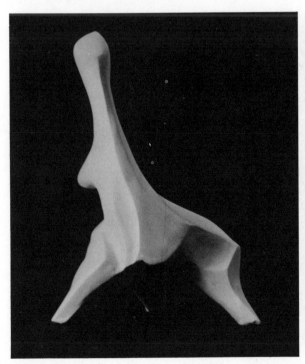

211. ANIMAL FORM, *Tom Harris*. Styrene.

212. GEOMETRY, *Tom Harris*. Styrene.

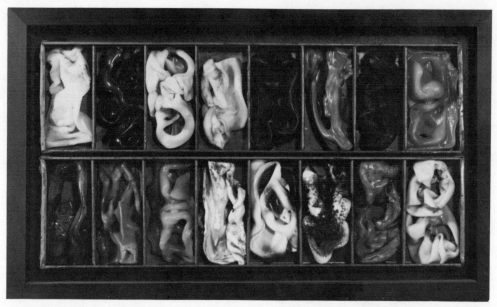

213. UNTITLED, *Robert Pierron*. Plastic objects such as cups, ice cube trays, and containers with inherent color were heated with a torch until their shapes sagged and became burnt and tortured. The resulting haphazard forms were then assembled into the compartments of a tool box tray.

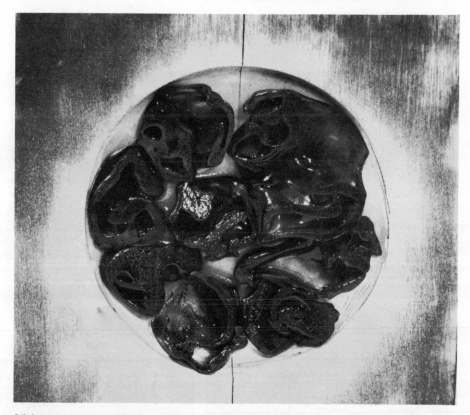

214. UNTITLED, *Robert Pierron*. Dark plastic cups were heated with an oxygen-acetylene torch until they sagged and bent. Placed in the circular form, they are symbolic of an embryo.

215. THE RACK, *David Packard*. Objects, string and wood encased in a heavy plastic bag.
Courtesy of the artist

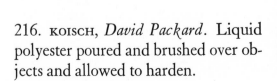

216. KOISCH, *David Packard*. Liquid polyester poured and brushed over objects and allowed to harden.

217. ORIXA, *Tereza D'Amico.* Feathers, stones, seed pods, coffee beans; careful study reveals a whole butterfly as the mouth, the skeleton of a fish as the nose, large thorny flowers as hands.

Courtesy, Museum of Contemporary Art of the University of São Paulo, Brazil

9 Mixed Materials

As the search for expressiveness with real materials in art continues, the artist's imagination freely roams his surroundings as subject and material for artistic statements. When Picasso turned a bicycle's handlebars and seat into a bull's head it was impossible for him to tell that he had set artistic thinking on a new road. Marcel Duchamp's placement of a bicycle wheel onto a wooden stool led to the present interest in kinetic art.

The artist's involvement with his materials will encourage him to use anything that comes within his emotional and physical grasp. It is difficult to predict what the standards of time will judge about the monumentality of the work. However, there is no doubt that the present era in the use of selected non-traditional materials has made an important twist in the path of art history.

In the examples that follow, each of the artists has combined an infinite range of materials in a single work of art. Completely unrelated objects have become related through their use in a new context, through repetition of shapes, textures, mass, density and colors. The examples run the gamut of the use of non-traditional art materials from some early Cubist to contemporary work. Paper, fabric, metal, plastic, and a variety of things from nature are combined.

The examples are offered to stimulate your own thoughts and techniques in creating art from anything.

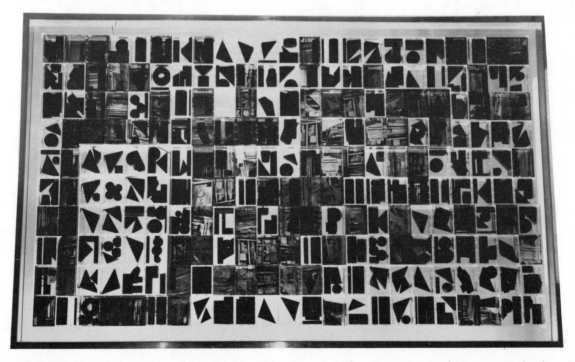

218. EXPANDING REFLECTION, *Louise Nevelson*. Silk-screening technique applied to plexiglass; wood shapes repeated within some of the boxes.
Courtesy, The Chase Manhattan Bank, New York

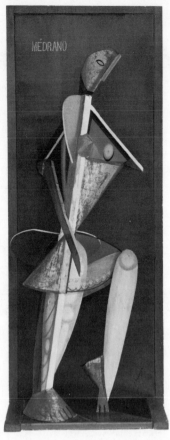

219. MEDRANO, *Alexander Archipenko* (1915)

Courtesy, The Solomon R. Guggenheim Museum, New York

220. BICYCLE WHEEL #2, *Marcel Duchamp* (1913)

Collection, Sidney Janis, New York

221. CHERRY PICTURE, *Kurt Schwitters* (1921)

Courtesy, The Museum of Modern Art, New York

219.—Early examples of mixed non-traditional materials in art include this relief collage consisting of painted tin, glass, wood and oilcloth.

220.—The original #1 version of this plain wire wheel mounted on a wood stool was the first construction made entirely from ready-made components. It was also the prototype of mobile sculptures. Whenever attendants were not looking, gallery goers reached out and spun the wheel.

221.—Collage of colored papers, fabrics, printed labels and pictures, pieces of wood, nails, etc. Schwitters is believed to have developed collage, using cast-off materials, into an art form that could rightfully stand up alongside painting. One historian says "... even today, there is scarcely a material, manner or meaning that Schwitters did not either invent or prophesy."

222.—This artist's work is believed to have been one of the influences upon contemporary artists in using real objects in their art.

223.—The artist has assembled items that to him symbolize and reflect the American way of life.

224.—Assortment of wood, cloth and objects from Mexico. A china doll sits within the cabinet; at the bottom, a printer's plate is nailed above a heart suspended on a bead chain.

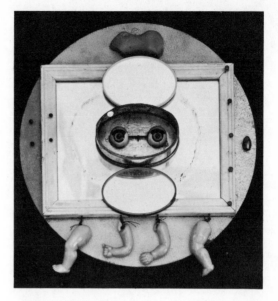

222. ANYBODY'S SELF-PORTRAIT, *George Cohen* (1953)
  Courtesy, Feigen Gallery, Chicago

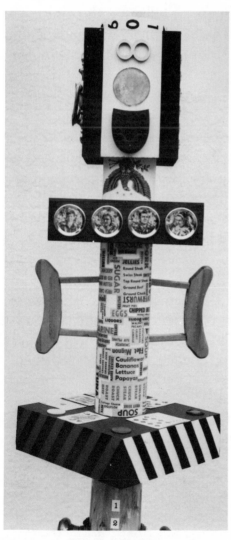

223. U.S. TOTEM, *Ivan Majdrakoff* (1967)
  Courtesy, The Arleigh Gallery, San Francisco

224. MONUMENT TO EVERYBODY, *Gordon Wagner* (1967)
  Courtesy of the artist

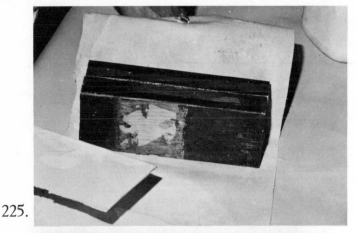

225.

226.

227.

228.

Artist Ralph Arnold demonstrates on this page the materials and techniques for achieving his construction shown on the facing page.

225.—He begins with a base made from two pieces of old two-by-four pine glued and nailed together. (If the wood surface does not lend itself to the finished product he has in mind, he covers it with artist's canvas simply by adhering the canvas to the wood with polymer glue and pulling it taut. This surface can later be painted with oils or acrylics.)

226.—Gears, typewriter keys, nails and any tools necessary for bending and hammering are used. The construction grows according to how the materials relate to one another, rather than by any sketch or preformed idea.

227.—When attached to the base, many pieces protrude above and beyond the block's surface. Some are bent around the corners to relate all the sides together.

228.—After items are assembled, color may be used for backgrounds and for accents. Mr. Arnold prefers to use acrylic paints because they dry quickly and the colors are bright and bold.

229. KEY MOVEMENT, *Ralph Arnold*. The finished construction.

230. BODY FACTORY, *Ralph Arnold*. A collage of many materials, using illustrations from medical textbooks, with gears symbolizing the mechanization of man.

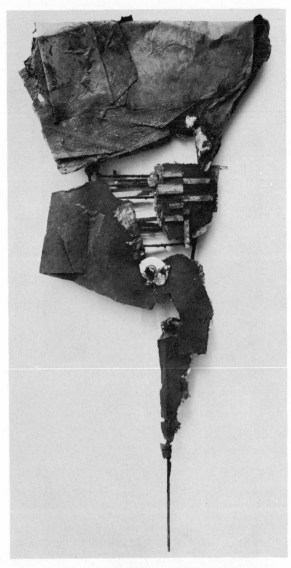

232. MACBETH, *Robert Mallary*. Cloth and wood with polyester resin.

Courtesy, Allan Stone Gallery, New York

231. JOUSTER, *Robert Mallary*. Wood, steel, fiberglass, sand and rags. A sense of despair is conveyed by use of decayed materials made permanent by the use of polyester resins.

Courtesy, Allan Stone Gallery, New York

233. STANDING FIGURE AS MONSTRANCE #1, *David Packard*. Polyester resin is employed here as the adherent and glazing polymer medium for scraps of wood, fabric, paper, bronze and ready-made objects.

Collection, William and Noma Copley, New York
Photo courtesy of the artist

234. CALLIOPE (WIDOW), *David Packard*. Steel, plastic, telephone book, nautical woolen mask, thread and other items.

Collection, Mr. and Mrs. Robert Mayer, Winnetka, Illinois
Photo courtesy of the artist

235. SNACK TRAY, *Robert Pierron*. Tray, knife and fork, ceramic faces and sliced pressed wood for crackers.

236. SEWING MACHINE, *Ivan Majdrakoff*. An example of the Funk Art movement of 1967 which has been called slickly crude, deliberately vulgar and somewhat funny. Funk art is visual double-talk; it makes fun of itself, though often it is deadly serious.

Courtesy, The Arleigh Gallery, San Francisco

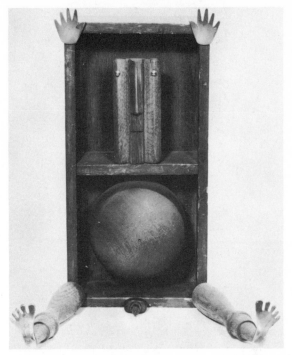

237. SCULPTAGE, *William Bowie*. Wall sculpture of steel coated with photographs.
Courtesy, The Sculpture Studio, Inc., New York

238. I SURRENDER, DEAR, *Robert Pierron*. Wooden box, wooden egg, tool handles (for legs), wooden violin tuning key and other wood fragments.

239. THE HEADACHE, *Wayne McGhie*. Practice golf balls cut in half and mounted on board with door cut in it; a box holding a plaster face is set onto the back.
Student, Deerfield High School

240. A PORTRAIT OF GEORGE, *Rubin Steinberg*. Heavy rope, wire coils, gears. Tiny metal parts are set in a bed of transparent polymer medium and seem to float on the surface in the semicircles made by the coils.

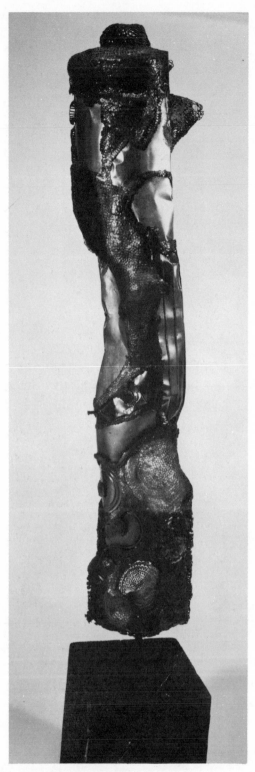

241. VERTIGO LANDSCAPE, *Seymour Locks*.
Wood and metal.
Courtesy, San Francisco Museum of Art

242. MOTHER AND CHILD #2, *Eve Garrison*.
Pieces of packing cartons, foam rubber,
fabric, labels, string and miscellany.

243. SPACE BOX, *Ralph Arnold*. Parts from a toy space kit, maps, pins and ping-pong ball on a golf tee are assembled inside an old sewing machine case that has been decorated in the space theme.

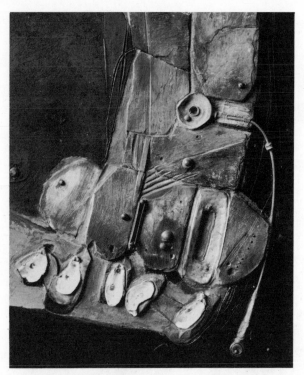

244. SLATES AND SHELLS, *Jaap Wagemaker*
Courtesy, Galerie Delta, Rotterdam

245. SOLAR A/1, *Sergio Lanzavecchia*
Courtesy, Galleria L'88, Rome

246. AGE OF CYBERNETICS, *Harry Dix*.
Wood and metal parts from machinery.
Courtesy, Bertha Schaefer Gallery, New York

247. LA PORTE ETROITE, *Hiquily*. Metal hand door knocker on weathered wood that has been painted.
Courtesy, Galerie Claude Bernard, Paris

248. SIBLINGS, *Alfonso Ossorio*. Glass eyes, shells, bone parts, pearls, broken mirrors, knobs, buttons, etc., set in a mixture of polymer medium and urea-base white glue on a wood panel.

Courtesy of the artist

Glue Chart

Materials to be glued	White glue	Resin glue	Polymer medium (acrylic emulsion)	Plastic resin urea base	Water-proof glue	Epoxy cement	Epoxy metal cement	House-hold glue	Contact cement	Rubber cement
Wood to wood	X	X		X	X					
Plastic to wood	X	X		X	X				X	
Wood outdoors				X	X					
Metal to wood	X	X				X	X		X	
China and glass						X		X		
Paper to paper and cardboard	X	X	X							X
Paper and cloth	X	X	X					X		
Cloth with wood	X	X	X					X		
Leather and wood	X	X	X						X	
Rubber to wood or metal						X	X	X	X	
Plastics, vinyls		X	X	X				X		
Collagraph items				X	X					
Glazing, preserving, sealing			X							
Stone and concrete to other items						X				
Rubber										X
Plastic foams		X	X	X				X	X	
Adding textures such as sand, stones, beads	X	X	X	X						
Metal to metal						X	X		X	

Always read and follow labels and manufacturers' directions.

Use of the glues as suggested in this chart is based on experience and knowledge, but it is not guaranteed. Individual experimentation with materials is recommended.

When gluing dissimilar materials, determine whether they are porous or non-porous. For example, porous materials are cloth, paper, cardboard, brick, wood and leather; non-porous materials are glass, metal, china, hard and soft plastics and rubber. Generally, when combining porous and non-porous materials, you should use the adhesive recommended for the non-porous material.